FEED THE WORLD FOR *Almost* FREE, FOREVER.

How We Can Use Recycled Plastic Containers to Build Greenhouses to End World Hunger NOW.

By Randall Putala

© 2009 World Hunger Team, LLC

ISBN-10 0-615-30455-9
ISBN-13 978-0-615-30455-7

www.WorldHungerTeam.com

First Edition, Sept. 2009

Table of Contents

Foreword 5
Overview 8
Chapter 1 - How The World Grows Food 13
Chapter 2 - The Five Components of Growing Food 16
Chapter 3 - What About Existing Charities? 20
Chapter 4 - Details of the WHT Plan 23
Chapter 5 - Plastics Recycling: A Cloudy Past - And Present 27
Chapter 6 - Our Sorting & Storage Solution 32
Chapter 7 - The Transformation: Converting "Recyclers" into "Reclamation Experts" 36
Chapter 8 - Putting the Training Into Action 39
Chapter 9 - Where Does The Plastic Go From Here? 46
Chapter 10 - Build Greenhouses 52
Chapter 11 - Mankind Needs Buildings of All Types 57
Chapter 12 - WHT Expanded Role: Housing 63
Chapter 13 - Current Conditions and Resources in Target Communities 67
Chapter 14 - The WHT Building Concepts 69
Chapter 15 - Controlling Temperatures within the Greenhouses 77
Chapter 16 - Fuel for Cooking and Heating 84
Chapter 17 - The 4-Greenhouse "POD" 87
Chapter 18 - Buildings: Unlimited Possibilities; Unlimited Challenges 89
Chapter 19 - Macro Farming - The Key To Large-Scale Hunger Relief 97
Chapter 20 - Water: The Key To Everything 99
Chapter 21 - Growing Food 111
Chapter 22 - The Basics: Soil 113
Chapter 23 - The Basics: Crops 120
Chapter 24 - Sprouts: Quick Food for the Neediest of Areas 129
Chapter 25 - Bread: The Cornerstone of Life 132
Chapter 26 - Other Growing Methods: Hydroponics 136
Chapter 27 - Fertilization, Pesticides and Pollination 138
Chapter 28 - Feed the Hungry 141
Chapter 29 - Medical Needs in Remote Villages 147
Chapter 30 - The Role of Technology & Science 151
Chapter 31 - WHT Implementation by Phases 160
Chapter 32 - Social Issues 162
Chapter 33 - WHT Participation Roles 165
Chapter 34 - National Database of Recyclables 170
Chapter 35 - WHT Operating Philosophy and Ethical Platform 172
Chapter 36 - Purpose in Life 176
Chapter 37 - WHT Rules of Order 179
Chapter 38 - WHT Financials 182
Chapter 39 - WHT Expanded Role: Helping the Homeless 184
Chapter 40 - Three Start-Up Levels 188
Chapter 41 - WHT Timetable for Implementation 190
Chapter 42 - Call To Action: What is YOUR Role? 193
Credits and Contacts 196

Foreword

We each have our jobs in life, as well as our goals. Your job may be to become the best teacher / firefighter / homemaker / sales rep or engineer in the world. Or your goal may be to climb Mount Everest, to build a better mousetrap, or to coach your child's softball team to the state championship. Jobs and goals are often unrelated, but they all contribute to fulfilling our unique definition of a successful life.

While we are reaching for our personal goals and leading our everyday lives, we often get asked to do side jobs. The goal of performing these side jobs may be to bring in more money for our family, to help out a friend, to help out the community, or simply to fill out the day and make life more personally rewarding.

World Hunger Team (WHT) became my side job in 2008, and I really can't tell you why; it just did. That 'side job', simply put, is to solve world hunger.

Laugh if you feel so inclined, roll your eyes, or write me off as another 'loose nut' in the great hardware store of life. But millions - literally millions of people around the world - are not laughing. They're dying. And the sad part is that they're dying for lack of a single tomato or potato or cucumber. They're dying for lack of a single morsel of food.

They're dying because the environment around them has ceased to provide nourishment. The blessed resources of mother earth have been disabled in their region, and the miraculous combination of rain / soil / seed is no longer growing food to feed their families. Yes, there are emergency responders - hundreds of fine charitable organizations that are addressing the need as best they can. But people continue to die because the delivery trucks from the relief charities can't be there every day - or they simply have no more food to distribute.

How great is the need? According to the website for Heifer International[1], a hunger relief organization based in Little Rock, AR:

> • More than 500 million people are living in "absolute poverty" and more than 15 million children die of hunger every year.

[1] *http://www.heifer.org*

- The World Health Organization estimates that one-third of the world population is underfed and another third is starving.

- In the United States, 46 percent of African-American children and 49 percent of Latino children are considered chronically hungry.

Our goal at WHT is to build food-growing resources - i.e., greenhouses, hot houses, irrigation beds, water storage tanks, barns, chicken coops, etc. - in the areas of greatest needs. We will do this using ordinary trash found in every American's garbage cans: plastic bottles, caps, packaging and other plastic materials that are currently piling up in landfills across our nation and throughout our oceans - polluting our environment and benefiting no one. We will harness these materials: capture them, recycle them, convert them into building materials, and use these materials to build growing facilities.

These buildings will be permanent installations, and they will be built in the areas of greatest need. These greenhouses, hot houses, farm buildings, and community buildings will be used to grow, prepare and store food, maintain livestock, and provide sustenance for people in need for generations to come. And we will accomplish this all by uniting the talents of top individuals, scientists, farmers, and companies across America.

WHT is an effort of 'we the people' - a concerned and caring nation that is looking for answers - people who are more than willing to work for a better tomorrow. People who will provide the answers and manpower needed to solve the world's problems. And they'll do it the old fashioned way: by rolling up their sleeves and getting the job done. Just as our ancestors united in the times of our nation's greatest needs, we can unite to actually make a difference in the world today. We have so much talent, such phenomenal technology, and such amazing resources, surely we can bring it all together for the good of the world.

Yes, you may say, there are plenty of excellent hunger-relief charities in the world, so why start another one? As you can read in the pages of your daily newspaper or view on the nightly news, the needs of the world are growing rapidly - but the response is not keeping pace, despite the best efforts of philanthropists around the globe.

As you will see in the pages of this book, there are new ways of doing things that are in practice today, things that are actually working; we simply need to roll these ideas out worldwide. There are other ideas, perhaps not yet realized, that we can test and implement. Combined with centuries of knowledge and proven expertise, these new ideas can make a huge difference in solving the hunger problems of our world.

I believe there is a huge base of people across our nation that want to help, but don't know how to get started. Some may have great knowledge, but don't know how to share it. Some may have tremendous technical skills but don't know how to apply them. Some may have economic needs of their own, but they have knowledge, time, energy and the will to participate.

These are all people who can help solve world hunger, people like you and me, like your friends, neighbors and co-workers. All we need is a way to connect and get involved. The goal of WHT is to be the conduit that brings all of these people together, to harness the world's most massive pool of talent, resource and materials to tackle specific objectives in a timely and targeted response. Our mission is to provide a specific and simplified action plan that is easily implemented and monitored - and one that is permanent. It can be done. It must be done. And it will be done, if we start humbly and grow nobly.

We can accomplish this by keeping things simple, easy, and harmonious:

The simpler	The better
The fewer moving parts	Less to break or go wrong
The less biodegradable the parts	Less to decompose or rust over time
The more basic the design	The easier to install and maintain
The more we assist natural processes	The greater the likelihood of success.

If this concept germinates an idea in your mind, you understand the mission. You know what your contribution can be. Write it down. Come back tomorrow and elaborate on it. Keep it in the back of your mind and dwell on it from time to time. This is how the WHT mission can become your mission, and how your time, talent and resources can benefit the world. I urge you to listen to your calling, and listen to your heart. It beats in rhythm with the heartbeat of humanity.

-Randall Putala

Overview

Good morning friends, neighbors and fellow travelers in this process called life.

Hunger is overtaking the world. Of this, there can be no denial.

At World Hunger Team (WHT), our goal is to be able to say the three sweetest words a hungry person wants to hear: "lunch is served." We want to create an environment whereby we can say this to hundreds - thousands - even millions of people around the world every day. After reaching this goal, our next goal is being able to say "breakfast is served," and "dinner is served." Everything else is superfluous. Everything else is just so much hot air - fluff - good intentions - enthusiastic repartee without substance. You can talk and talk and talk, but the guy on the street or out on the hot tundra with no shoes, no job, no money, and no hope, is looking for one thing: his next meal. And he can't eat good intentions.

The hungry inhabitants of our planet are dying by the thousands every day. They are looking to us for help. They have no resources, no bank account, no local grocery store, no neighbor they can run to and ask for a handout. Their environment has largely turned hostile; food will not grow due to lack of water, animals cannot survive for lack of ground cover and water to sustain them. Most of the 'fallback' support that we may enjoy here in the United States is gone - there are no optional resources that starving people can rely on day after day, week after week.

Even in the prosperous United States, hunger is knocking on many doors. Relief organizations are stretched to the max and generosity is running out in favor of protecting one's own family and well being. We may feel charitable on special occasions, and that certainly helps; giving the poor guy on the street one free meal a year on Thanksgiving may make the well-to-do feel among us feel pretty darn special. And on that one day, it makes the poor and destitute people feel good as well. But on Friday morning, it's a new day: that same guy needs another meal... and another, every day thereafter. And guess what? He's got friends - lots of them.

That's because the number of homeless, hungry, and destitute people in the world is rising at an astronomical rate. The models on which developed nations have built worldwide economic and agronomic success are simply not keeping up with human needs in the 21st century. The Beatles had it correct when they sang, "Obladi Oblada, life goes on.[2]" Life will go on; families will continue to have babies, babies will continue to grow into children, children will continue to grow into men and women, and the cycle will repeat itself as it has for all of eternity. Food is a non-negotiable component of this process, and we as the sentient citizens of this planet will either provide the food that the world needs, or we will not. The choice is ours to make either through a formal declaration or by avoiding the issue, but the ever-expanding lot of humanity will not have that choice; they will either live or die by our decision.

A Simple Answer to a Complex Problem

WHT is taking a radical overview to the hunger problem. In short, we have made it our mission to create a more lasting and permanent solution to world hunger. The process we will follow to grow limitless quantities of food is to:

a. Collect recyclable plastic, i.e. milk jugs, soft drink bottles, medicine bottles, etc.- on a large, nationwide scale.

b. Maintain the integrity of the collected items through a simple, numerical tracking system, i.e. keeping all "1" plastic separate from "2", "3", "4", etc.

c. Create high-quality building materials out of the recycled plastic, strengthened with the latest technology in UV-resistance.

d. Develop simple, easily-constructed greenhouses, hothouses and other growing structures out of these materials.

e. Grow vegetables, grains, sprouts, and fruits within these buildings

[2]*Lyrics © 1968 EMI Records.*

to provide a renewable, sustainable food supply in communities of need.

Our overriding goal is to feed the world's population on an ongoing, permanent basis. The four parts of our motto explain it all:

- We <u>recycle plastic</u> to <u>build greenhouses</u> to <u>grow food</u> to <u>feed the hungry</u>.

- We propose to dramatically raise the perceived importance and value of recycling individual types of plastic by numbers.

- We want to rally the U.S. public on a grass-roots level.

- We aim to unite them within a common cause for the greater good of mankind: feeding the human population on an ongoing, permanent basis.

Everyone - Regardless of Age, Health, Wealth, or Experience - Can Participate

WHT proposes to harness and combine the resources of each and every concerned American. We want people of all ages, backgrounds, and capabilities to join with us and demonstrate to the world that we are good and caring people. We want to collect the combined knowledge of people from all walks of life:

- From the horticultural skills of farmers in Iowa to the manufacturing expertise of a contractor in Florida

- From the chicken-raising skills of a 12-year old boy in Pennsylvania to the gardening skills of a grandmother in Oregon

- From the design skills of an architect in Tennessee to the plastics engineering skills of a chemist in New York

- From the transportation skills of an Army logistics officer stationed in Alaska to the plastic sorting skills of school children in Michigan

- From the production expertise of the largest consumer goods companies in the nation to the homeless people who collect empty containers

Everyone has something to contribute to WHT, regardless of their status in life or income level. This contribution has nothing to do with money, it has to do with knowledge, expertise, and the desire to pitch in to help. If your sleeves roll up, you're qualified.

So many charities ask for your help in only one way: money. And that's a necessary approach, especially if the need is for more medical research, laboratory testing, financial support to the indigent, etc. There is nothing wrong with these charities, and they need and deserve your support. But WHT is different. We aim to be one of the few charitable organizations that literally every American, regardless of age, health, wealth, or experience, can actively participate in. As we like to say, *"We don't want your cash, we want your trash."*

Conversely, WHT is not just about giving; it's also about receiving.

Everyone has something to gain from being a member of WHT:

- You gain the satisfaction of knowing that you are helping to feed starving people around the world, and even in your home community.

- You gain friendship and the camaraderie of being part of a worldwide movement, the "WPA" corps of the 21st century, if you will.

- You gain knowledge, as all developments, techniques, and success stories are shared worldwide over the Internet.

- You gain a global perspective that cannot be obtained through the newspaper or TV; you will be dealing with people from all corners of the earth.

- You gain sustenance; while you may not personally need a source for your next meal, your neighbor might. By helping to develop the WHT chapter in your own community, you will be providing a local food resource for those in need.

As you read through the chapters of this book, let your mind roam free to consider what your role in WHT could be. The answers that form in your mind may surprise you - but capture and 'plant' them, by writing them down in the back pages of this book. Over time, they could grow into something very interesting. Like the magic beans that Jack planted in his yard, they could be the key to discovering *your* next chapter in life, as well.

Chapter 1 - How the World Grows Food

For tens of thousands of years prior to the development of our modern industrialized society, local food production was a mandatory fact of life; if you didn't grow it, you didn't eat it. As time progressed, enterprising farmers started growing more than the local community needed, and they began to export their goods to other villages, other counties and eventually other countries. These exported goods often became rare commodities and commanded a high price because the local communities were unable to grow the same crops in their locale.

Eventually the world came to rely on the availability of these exported goods on a continued basis. Bananas and other tropical fruits were available in the northern regions year-round. This change in food supply and culture came about due to one key word: logistics.

The food industry figured out the logistics of harvesting bananas in tropical countries and delivering them just-in-time for consumption to all points of the world. Eventually the same process was repeated for lettuce, oranges, peaches, squash, and so on. The demand for specific commodities to be delivered in specific quantities to specific locations was effectively met by the food industry - and it was met with extreme efficiency. This was and remains a marvel of industrialized society.

The key component that is required for this highly efficient food delivery system to function properly is capital. The participants in our global food production and distribution system must receive a fair price for their goods, or they simply won't keep delivering them; no money, no honey.

The costs to produce food in today's economy are skyrocketing out of control; the cost of fertilizers and insecticides is increasing each year, the cost of fuel needed to transport the goods is at a record high, and the costs of labor needed to grow, process, package and transport these goods are all rising each and every day.

The sad reality is that our global economy is fragmenting on an ever-accelerating pace. The 'haves' continue to expand their wealth, and the 'have-nots' are facing a spiraling decline in their economic futures. The chances of our global economy repairing itself and self-correcting to a sustainable level are not good.

We cannot rely on our established food procurement system to continue to meet the world's needs, because the world cannot support the food industry's minimum level of operational needs. The entire system is being propped up by credit, and like the proverbial balloon, it could soon "pop." But if it does pop, the distribution chain will not disappear, it will simply reconfigure itself into survival mode. The system will continue to support the 'haves' because they will bring ready and plentiful cash to the table. It will NOT continue to support the 'have-nots', because they won't have the cash needed to pay the tab. It's as simple as that.

The soup kitchens of the 1920s were an embarrassment to the United States government, but they were pretty darn important to the hungry man on the street. For many families, 'going on the dole' was the only way to survive until the economic system recovered its ability to provide jobs to everyone who wanted to work.

But soup kitchens are only a temporary patch. In the great depression of 1928, it took this nation almost 10 years to get back on its feet, and perhaps another 15 years beyond that that to experience anything resembling prosperity.

How long will it take for us - and the world - to reverse the current trend of declining prosperity and rising hunger? No one can accurately answer that question, of course. But bear in mind that the world population is four times larger today than it was in 1928. There are FOUR TIMES as many mouths to feed globally. How many soup kitchens can we establish worldwide?

If you view the world's population economically, roughly ¼ are the 'haves' and ¾ are the 'have nots.' Are 25% of the world's people going to be willing or able to fund soup kitchens for the other 75%? It is unreasonable to expect the wealthy people of the world to give their wealth away to the non-wealthy.

History will prove that, in fact, the OPPOSITE has happened. When the world goes into survival mode, people hunker down and hold on to what they have - and sharing becomes less of a priority than helping your own family hold onto what they have. When food becomes a precious commodity, people will naturally horde what they can and share even less of it than they have in the past. Over time, the situation gets worse, not better.

An interesting phenomenon takes place when people cannot afford to feed their family. Families find alternative ways to get food. They grow vegetables in the back yard (remember "victory gardens" during World War II?) Local communities band together into 'farm collectives' to exchange food: the dairy farmer exchanges his dairy products for vegetables; the cattle rancher exchanges beef for milk and vegetables. Money does not enter into equation; rather, fresh food becomes the gold standard - because people can live without money, but they cannot live without food.

Chapter 2 - The Five Components of Growing Food

Food is the primary commodity of mankind. And the beauty of food is that, with a little bit of care and guidance, it grows by itself. Amazingly, the world can produce all the food that the people living on it can consume - and more.

The process of growing food requires five things:

1. **Soil**. The entire world is made of rich, vibrant soil. It's underneath your feet right now. It's free.

2. **Water**. It falls down out of the sky every now and then. It's free.

3. **Seeds**. They're in the foods you eat every day. One tomato has between 50 to 500 of them, depending on variety.

4. **Fertilizer**. It's made out of waste products. Waste is produced by all species everywhere, every day, naturally. It's free.

5. **Light**. The sun rises every morning, and sets every night. It provides all the light needed to grow food, and it's free.

Of course, the missing component of all of this is management. Plants need a little TLC to make sure the five items above are brought together in a logical and consistent way. Lots of people around the world have this expertise. From three year old kids to 103 year old great-grandparents, the collective people of the world know a LOT about growing food. All we need to do is bring these five elements - and the knowledge of the world's gardeners together - to grow enough food to feed the world.

The other component that is critical to reaching the optimal output of food is environmental control. We at WHT propose to create the ideal conditions for plants to survive, using recycled plastic to build growing facilities.

This book provides a simplified overview of how we will accomplish this; it will be up to the engineers and architects who become WHT volunteers to draft the exact specifications. It will be up to the botanists and horticulturalists to determine the correct variety of plants to grow and the correct nutrients and fertilizers to use. Our goal is to consistently maximize the food output of each growing facility that we install.

These growing facilities will provide ongoing sustenance to local communities, regardless of the weather, and regardless of the frequency and quantity of local rainfall. However, we will not forsake traditional large-scale farming techniques. Rather, we will supplement these techniques through rainwater collection facilities and gravity-fed irrigation pipes. This will bring some degree of control and predictable success to large-field food production.

In summary, the goals of WHT are to:

a. Provide a reliable, affordable, permanent source of food in areas of the world with the greatest need.

b. Enlist the joint efforts of thousands - even millions - of people from all walks of life around a common goal.

c. Harness the unique talents of individuals of all ages and all backgrounds, and share the best information globally.

d. Educate the nations of the world about the hunger issue, and enlist them in providing a permanent solution to the problem.

e. Learn and improve the food production process continually, using knowledge gleaned from the worldwide WHT installations.

When the world is eating three square meals a day, turf battles and war don't somehow don't seem as important. Life can go on, for everyone. We can - and must - replace the existing food distribution system with a localized agrarian system that meets the specific food requirements of each community in need. That is the mission of World Hunger Team - and it is a need that we believe we have developed an effective system to meet.

Why bother with the needs of people we don't know?

The question facing any charitable organization is, "Am I my brother's keeper?" In other words, why is it our responsibility to feed people half way around the world - shouldn't their government or their churches or their charitable organizations be helping them? And the answer is, yes they should be. But the resources in many of these countries are so limited, or their economic and political systems are so restricting, they don't know what to do next. Because we are rational, caring human beings, it is in our nature to attempt to share our success with these people.

Abraham Maslow addressed the question of life's purpose with his famous theory on the hierarchy of needs. The following illustration shows how he ranked the lifetime needs of humans:

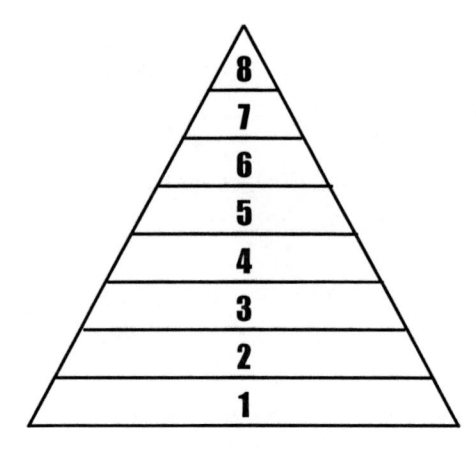

1) Physiological hunger, thirst, bodily comforts, etc.
2) Safety / security: out of danger
3) Belongingness and Love: affiliate with others, be accepted
4) Esteem: to achieve, be competent, gain approval and recognition
5) Cognitive: to know, to understand, and explore
6) Aesthetic: symmetry, order and beauty
7) Self-actualization: to find self-fulfillment and realize one's potential
8) Transcendence: to help others find self-fulfillment and realize their potential

- At level 1, the starving people of the world cannot meet even the most basic needs in their lives.

- We who have so much to be thankful for can often hover in levels 3 and below, content to enjoy the fruits of our labors.

- Many will strive for level 4 and desire the approval of their peers.

- As one ages in life, the tendency is to travel the world in search of beauty, art and knowledge as found in levels 5 and 6.

- The act of charitable giving and helping out those in need comes into full play in levels 7 and 8: we want to find ourselves and achieve our definition of success, by helping those who cannot help themselves regardless of their best efforts. We want to share what is good in our lives, with others.

We believe that there is a great longing among the American population to reach levels 7 and 8 - to come to know ourselves as unique individuals, to find a purpose in life, to share the gifts of knowledge, understanding, caring and sustenance with the world. By understanding our own self worth and sharing the gifts and talents we have been given, in a unified cause toward a common goal, we can find true peace within ourselves.

The forces of the world may be misaligned and heading toward catastrophic ends, but we do not have to be burdened with them. By jointly working together to help the truly needy people of the world, we can find answers to our own needs and achieve lifelong satisfaction.

Some find this satisfaction in religion or faith, some find it in science, some find it in philanthropy. Our philosophy is that we as individuals can apply our own definition of satisfaction through the efforts of the World Hunger Team. And, we can do it by participating in whatever way we are called.

Chapter 3 - What About Existing Charities - Aren't They Already Serving Needy Communities Around The World?

There are plenty of existing charities sending billions of dollars in aid into the impoverished areas of the world every year. But is the need solved? Is the need diminishing? No. In fact, the opposite is occurring. Population growth is on the rise in all corners of the globe. But is capitalization and infrastructure funding rising at the same pace? Not in anyone's wildest dreams. The traditional economic structure of growth and capitalization cannot keep pace with the world's needs. As mentioned previously, there is a huge and growing gap between the "haves" and the "have-nots".

Charitable nations can make contributions to minimize the effects of this gap, but the charitable nations are losing their grip on the peak of the financial mountain. Manufacturing has largely moved off-shore to cheaper markets, so the tremendous financial windfall that the world's top nations once held is slipping away. So the core funding for charitable donations - surplus capital of the major nations of the world - is shifting to other countries, slowly but surely. And the beneficiaries of that shift have their own interests at stake, not the world's needs.

Why WHT is Unique

Another way to look at WHT is that we are not a charity that delivers food as a temporary one-time donation. Our goal is to help alleviate a permanent and largely unsolved problem. Think of WHT as a SWAT team that comes in on a temporary one-time building mission, with the goal of making headway on a permanent solution to the problem.

It is true that the humanitarian charities of the world are already doing incredible things to improve food production and living conditions among the poor in every nation of the world. The list reads like an honor roll of the world's greatest charitable organizations:

- UNICEF
- United Nations World Food Programme
- Oxfam
- Project Hope
- Feeding America (formerly America's Second Harvest)
- CARE
- Catholic Relief Services
- Feed the Children
- Heifer Project International
- Many more - too many to list individually

Have these charities 'got it wrong' and is WHT opposed to their actions? Absolutely not! We applaud their efforts wholeheartedly. Our goal is to work hand-in-hand with any and all other charity groups in a collaborative effort to make an impact on world hunger.

To say that one charity is 'competing' with another is ludicrous. Think of each charity as a beacon of light in a world full of darkness. The tremendous effort of these charities in contributing to the solution is overwhelming and magnificent, yet the combined impact of these fine organizations is dwindling in the shadow of the resurgent and ever-growing problem. Established charities simply cannot meet the staggering need that our world presents today. Will these charities welcome the efforts of WHT? We can only hope so, and we hope that they will be among the first to make recommendations as to where our assistance is needed most.

Challenges Ahead

If money were limitless and volunteers abundant, the existing hunger charities of the world could generate amazing results in solving world hunger. But with a tightening economy, skyrocketing population growth, and a growing disparity between the 'haves' and 'have-nots', charitable donations and volunteerism are declining.

Whether or not WHT can overcome these limitations remains to be seen. We believe we have a good chance of growing our contribution to the world's needs, because we are attempting to enlist the help of a wide swath of society - from rich to poor, from young to old. And the unquestionable answer to "does the world need a WHT" is "yes - of course." We may fail, but not for lack of need, desire or commitment. And if we succeed, even to a limited degree, the world will be better off for our efforts.

Chapter 4 - Details of the WHT Plan

As stated in the overview, there are four primary categories of the WHT plan:

1. Recycle plastic
2. Build greenhouses
3. Grow food
4. Feed the hungry

Let us take a closer look at each one of these categories. The details involved in each step are massive and some may be hard-to-follow, but each is critical in the grand plan. To the laymen, these steps may seem too intricate, but to the tradesmen - the people who live their lives within each of these disciplines, this is heady stuff. It is our goal at WHT to involve the nation's experts in refining the details in each of these areas. As the plan involves and the details are refined to their most pure and basic elements, a highly effective system will evolve.

1. Recycle Plastic

Plastic packaging materials have benefited mankind in countless ways. They benefit our food supply system by preserving the freshness of foods for extended lengths of time, thus making the long-distance transportation of food possible by easing transportation and preserving freshness of the items we consume. The same properties that make these plastics so beneficial to us can further extend their usefulness in society. Rather than sit idle in landfills, or even as pollutants of the land or oceans, plastics can continue to serve a valued purpose if properly recycled and re-used.

The entire operating premise of WHT rests on one key fact: plastic does not decompose rapidly, at least not if it is protected from the ultraviolet (UV) rays of the sun. Technically all plastic DOES decompose, but at an unbelievably slow rate. You've all heard the story about a plastic bottle that is buried in a landfill: come back in 1,000 years and it will still be there - virtually unchanged. That one analogy led to the concept behind WHT: why not convert the plastic bottle into a building block, and use that building block to create a structure? In theory, that structure could be there for 1,000 years or more - virtually unchanged!

If you think about how much plastic the average household uses in a year, the total is staggering. In my own household of 5 people - 2 adults and 3 kids - we fill three large drums with recyclable material each and every week. This includes aluminum cans, tin cans, newspapers and glass, of course. But the number of plastic bottles and containers we generate is truly amazing. If our household's plastic waste could somehow be converted into bricks, rebar, window frames, windows, doors and hardware, just one year's total output could likely be enough to build a small shed. Over the course of 10 years, it would probably be enough material to build a garage. And over the course of 30 or 40 years, we would probably generate enough material to build an entire house. Imagine that: the occupants of one house, generating enough plastic materials from their trash, to build ANOTHER house in a far-off land.

Now, imagine that this was somehow possible - that the majority of the plastic generated by households around the world - was used to construct new buildings. The world could see millions of new homes, schools, churches and service buildings where none exist today. Or the plastic could simply be recaptured and reused to make new packaging materials. Or on the other hand, we could do nothing and see hundreds of miles of new landfills, chock full of permanent waste plastic that is contributing nothing to society. Which application best serves the needs of mankind?

The basic premise of WHT is simple: collect recyclable plastic and put it to good use. Most people would be glad to donate these items, so for all intents and purposes the core components of our building materials are free. We can get all that we want, all that we can use. All we have to do is figure out what to do with it. And that is the core of the WHT mission:

- Find some very smart people with a wide range of skills
- Assemble a well-organized team to work together
- Harness a vast array of complex knowledge into a simple

> operational plan
- Develop the shortest, most inexpensive path from A (consumer waste) to B (permanent buildings)

Are Plastics a Problem in Today's Environment?

Plastic products and by-products are found everywhere in the world, and are used by people from all walks of life. When people are done using them, the plastics are discarded and eventually deposited in landfills and dumps. The same scrap materials are also found in fields, along highways, and throughout the oceans of the world. Plastic dust and residue are even found in the air we breathe, the food we eat, and in the water we drink. Plastics are taking over the environment, and unless something is done to reduce this problem, it may put a choke-hold on our existence.

Studies conducted in 2001 by the Algalita Marine Research Foundation[3], a non-profit organization based in California, showed that in parts of the northern Pacific Ocean, there were six times more plastic debris than zooplankton. The small bits of plastic that remain after photodegradation, (the breakdown of plastic caused by UV light from the sun) are called "nurdles" or "mermaid tears."

According to the web site www.GreenDaily.com, "Nurdles are the tiny plastic pieces that are used in molds to create everything from plastic packaging to doll's heads. So small are these oblong bits of plastic that they often fall through the cracks and out the doors of the trucks and factories that use them.

They end up in the ocean. Shrimp, turtles, lobsters, fish and birds have all ingested these little plastic pieces thinking they were food. But plastic is indigestible, so smaller creatures like shrimp and bass die from constipation and starvation. If they are consumed by larger sea creatures, before their own deaths those animals eventually develop blockages in their own digestive system."

Nurdles are not a small problem in today's environment. The GreenDaily web site states, "Sewer systems and waste water treatment facilities do not have a means of catching nurdles before they get to water. Greenpeace has found massive amounts of nurdles in the Indian

[3] www.algalita.org

Ocean, the Pacific Ocean, the Bay of Bengal, the Red Sea, and off the coast of the Philippines. Even the Atlantic is developing a bad case of the nurdle.

In 2007 California signed into law a bill that forces manufacturers to mind their nurdles. But nurdles remain a huge problem around the world. For every square mile of ocean about 13,000 bits of plastic are floating around according to the United Nations."

Clearly, plastic waste in our oceans is a problem that needs to be addressed by the world at large. According to the United Arab Emirates-based environmental scientist Mohammad Abu Al Aish, "Fish eat plankton, but when there is more plastic than plankton in the water, they may confuse it for food and eat it instead." And more often than not, plastic has fatal consequences for marine creatures. The United Nations Environment Program found that every year, plastic is accountable for the death of more than a million seabirds and more than 100,000 aquatic mammals such as whales, dolphins, and seals.

Aaron Bartholomew, assistant professor of biology at the American University of Sharjah in the UAE, considers plastic bags one of the greatest killers at sea. "Many endangered species of sea turtles mistake plastic bags for jellyfish. Once they swallow it, the bags block their digestive tract and they starve to death," he said.

With thousands of tons of waste plastic being dumped into our oceans every year, this debris has the potential to seriously damage the world's natural food chain if left unchecked. Our contention at World Hunger Team is that this very same plastic waste can be recycled and put to work in building greenhouses, community buildings, houses and more. By applying this waste plastic toward humanitarian goals, we can solve multiple problems at one time. By preventing a significant amount of this debris from reaching our oceans, we can help retain the natural balance of the world's food chain.

Chapter 5 - Plastics Recycling: A Cloudy Past - and Present

While most communities in America recycle plastic today, most do it somewhat ineffectively. That is not a criticism; it's a fact. Less than 10% of all post-consumer plastic is recycled, and many communities have to actually pay to have their recycled plastics hauled off. Why? Because the plastics are mixed, and can often NOT BE REUSED! The causes of this are many:

- Incompatible mix of plastic types in the recycling bins. Many consumers add plastics #3, 4, 5, 6 & 7 in the bin reserved for #1 and #2 exclusively - in essence 'polluting' the value of the properly-deposited #1 & #2 items.

- Lack of consumer knowledge of what is recyclable, what the numbers mean, and how to sort and recycle the various numbers of plastic.

- Limited uses for mixed-code recycled plastic; plastic reclamation is not as 'clean' a process as recycling aluminum, steel or glass.

- Limited knowledge of what byproducts the different numbers can make, and the unique strengths of 'pure plastics'.

- Limited capacity to collect, store, and recycle plastics by number. The challenge to get ANY plastic recycled or reused is huge; increasing the complexity of recycling plastics by number would likely decrease the overall consumer involvement - which is already incredibly low.

- Lower value in recycled plastic; not as much profit per lb. as aluminum or steel 'tin' cans.

The plastics industry came up with a great game plan many years ago: identify and mark the different types of plastic packaging with numbers, a Plastic Identification Code (PIC).

There are seven groups of plastic polymers, each with specific properties. The numbers 1 through 7 are used worldwide to identify the specific type of plastic used to manufacture the specific packaging item, (see table below). The PIC appears inside a three-chasing arrow recycling symbol, typically found on the bottom of most (but not all) plastic containers. The symbol is used to indicate whether the plastic can be recycled into new products.

Has this worked? Well, yes and no. Quiz your own knowledge of what the numbers mean, and what numbers are found on the plastic containers used in your household. *(HINT: unless you work in the plastics industry, chances are you'll miss one or two of these...)*

#1 PETE Polyethylene Terephthalate	Plastic soft drink, water, sports drink, mouthwash, ketchup and salad dressing bottles. Peanut butter, pickle, jelly & jam jars.
#2 HDPE High Density Polyethylene	Frosted milk, juice, cosmetics, shampoo, dish & laundry detergent bottles, yogurt and margarine tubs.
#3 VINYL or PVC	PVC, PVB, EVA Medical tubing, wire and cable insulation, film and sheet, construction products such as pipes, fittings, siding, floor tiles, carpet backing and window frames. NOT typically accepted by recycling programs!
#4 LDPE Low Density Polyethylene	Squeezable bottles such as honey and mustard bottles.
#5 PP Polypropylene	Ketchup bottles, yogurt containers and margarine tubs, medicine bottles.
#6 PS Polystyrene; GPPS, HIPS, EPS Foam	Compact disc jackets, food service applications, grocery store meat trays, foam egg cartons, cups, plates & cutlery. NOT typically accepted by recycling programs!
#7 OTHER Polycarbonate, Acrylic, ABS, Mixed Plastics	Three and five gallon reusable water bottles, some citrus juice and ketchup bottles.

When the plastics industry developed this identification schema many years ago, they figured that consumers would embrace it, and come to know by heart which plastics could be recycled and which could not, and also be willing to keep the recyclable items separate. In theory, it sounded great. The numbers would become etched in the minds of every consumer, and people would only recycle compatible types of plastic.

Of the two types of plastic that often ARE accepted by recycling centers (#1 Polyethylene Terephthalate ("PETE") and #2 High Density Polyethylene ("HDPE"), indicated with a #1 (PETE) or #2 (HDPE) on the bottom, does your recycling center sort the donated plastics by these numbers? Does your trash pick-up company or recycling center sort them out? Or do they mix everything into one common pool and assume that 'someone' down the line does the sorting? The answer may shock you: most plastic is NEVER sorted out to the core 7 levels. Only the #1 & #2 portion - generally the largest portion of donated plastic - is kept 'pure' by number. But the value - and the ability to reuse *other* numbered plastic as commercially-viable materials - rises dramatically if the batched recyclable plastic materials are kept impeccably pure by number.

The most desirable source of recyclable plastic is bottles. Plastic bottles typically contain beverages (juice, soda, water, alcohol), food items (sauces, dressings), cleaning products (window spray, cleaning solutions) or personal care products (shampoo, conditioner, hand cream.)

In essence, ALL plastic bottles and containers are recyclable. Clear plastics are generally more recyclable and sought after than colorized plastics. Clear bottles are usually separated from colorized bottles to maximize the value of the reclaimed materials.

The other plastic products that are typically less desirable for recycling include such items as tubs, which are wide and often have lids made of different material, (butter, whipped topping, cottage cheese, sour cream), brittle plastic or polystyrene (Styrofoam®) cups, jugs (e.g., detergent containers), hard plastic cosmetic jars (cold cream, skin care) etc. These items are typically made of a wide range of mixed plastic grades or resins: PETE (#1), HDPE (#2), PVC (#3), LDPE (#4), PP (#5), PS (#6), and other (#7). In most recycling situations, these items are considered less recyclable and less valuable, but in the context of WHT and our extreme sorting procedures, we believe we can make these items economically feasible to recycle, and structurally viable when reconstruded as building materials.

Plastic is the Most Complex Item in Your Recycling Bin!

One of the key advantages of recycling aluminum is the fact that there is really only one type of aluminum can. Be it a beer can, a soda can, or a juice can, you can pretty much feel the difference between an aluminum can and a 'tin' can (which is really made of tin-plated steel, if you want to get technical.) So keeping the aluminum content pure is a fairly simple task. And glass recycling? It's a breeze: you've got clear, brown and green, (with occasional exceptions such as blue.)

But can you tell the seven major categories of plastic apart at a glance? Not really! You need to look closely at the tiny number on the bottom of the container. It's about 1/16th of an inch high. It's typically a white embossing, on a white background. Only an eagle eye can spot the numbers, and only the most obsessive compulsive among us sorts the plastics in their recycling bin accordingly. Do you have 7 different plastics bins in your garage or basement? I know I don't! Just take a quick glance through the assortment of containers in the plastics bin at your local recycling center and you'll see why this is such a problem for the industry.

Why Do We Need to Sort the Plastics In The First Place?

When plastics are separated by number and kept in pure batches, (i.e. no mixing of the numbers) and melted down, the resulting plastic is virtually indistinguishable from the original components. And since the virgin material was made from oil, it has tremendous value.

Another little-known fact is that thermoplastics - another name for the numbered plastics used as packaging for the beverages and products we use every day - actually get _stronger_ when they are melted down and re-used. This is because the fibers of the plastic realign in the re-melting process to form a better union. So the building materials that we will make from the recycled pure plastic will actually have GREATER strength and functionality than if they were made from virgin plastic. Imagine the impact of this: not only are we re-using waste material, we're making it better as well!

When different types of plastics are melted together they tend to split like oil and water, and set in different layers. These separate layers or 'phase boundaries' cause structural weakness in the resulting material, meaning that the resulting product or 'polymer blends' are only useful in limited applications.

Another barrier to keeping the recycled product pure is the widespread use of dyes, fillers, and other additives in plastics. The polymer is generally too viscous or 'thick' to economically remove the fillers. Also, removing the dyes could damage the final product and render it structurally unusable. Clear plastic bottles have no dyes present, making them the 'purest of the pure' in terms of recycling potential. This is why we need to sort the plastic down to the single-digit number and maintain the purity of the sort. Further sorting of clear and color plastic may be necessary to maintain the proper luminosity, transparency or aesthetics of the final building materials.

Chapter 6 - Our Sorting and Storage Solution

There are many issues facing the plastics industry in its effort to improve their recycling track record:

- **Complexity**: there are seven different types of plastic that many people cannot tell apart.

- **Labeling**: there is poor or no identification on many products.

- **Mixed Usage**: most plastic containers use 2 or more types of plastic among its components.

- **Consumer misinformation or lack of knowledge**: few people truly know about the differences in plastic or why they should recycle in the first place.

- **Low value of the recycled plastic**: it's often cheaper for manufacturers to just buy virgin materials (and consume more oil in the process.)

- **Consumer apathy**: it's easier to just throw containers in the trash, or the attitude of "why is it my problem, anyway?"

- **Lack of funds for consumer training and education**: who wants to add more expense to packaging, when the economy is so tight?

With so many issues, how on earth is the industry ever going to solve its problems? And beyond that, how is World Hunger Team going to overcome these pre-existing issues and really start recycling plastic in significant volumes?

The answer is complex, but it has its origin in cleanliness and thoroughness. In order to make this entire proposition work, we have to establish a mindset that the items found in your trash can have extreme value - but only if they are treated with the respect they are due.

Look at an ordinary vitamin bottle, a prescription vial, or a clear sports drink bottle. These are all made of exceptionally durable plastic, and in theory you could use them over and over again for the next 10 or 20 years without them ever losing their shape or deteriorating in any way. Yet we as a society treat them as unusable after their initial use. Why do we do this? Primarily, it is because of hygiene issues: once a product comes into human contact, it is no longer hygienic to be reused in its original state. Structurally, it will not change very much over the next 1,000 years (unless exposed to the UV rays of the sun.) But because it touched your hands or lips, it cannot be reused. What a waste!

What if we just recycle the plastic and keep the separate types "pure" - won't that solve the problem? Well, yes - in theory. But the process of identifying and separating the plastic components found in the millions of different consumer brands and packages is too costly to make "pure" recycling possible, given the many issues identified above.

Recycling As We Know It Now is NOT the Answer

In order to solve the issue of separating the plastics and keeping the recycling batches 'pure', it's important to understand the difference between 'ordinary recycling' and true 'plastic reclamation.'

In ordinary recycling:

- Rinse your plastic bottles out once (or maybe not at all.)
- Leave significant traces of whatever was in the jug in the first place - milk, shampoo, laundry detergent, etc.
- Leave the label on the bottle, leave the cap and cap ring on the bottle; heck, if you put your cigarette out in the bottle, leave that in there, too; who's going to notice...
- Dump anything that is plastic - regardless of code - into the recycling bin that is clearly marked "#1 & #2 Plastic Only".
- What the hey... nobody's watching - go ahead and dump everything into one bin; you can still say you tried to be "green."
- Leave the final sort and/or clean-up to "them" - whoever "they" are - the people who pick up the recycling bin and have to deal with all of the junk inside.

Bear in mind that the vast majority of consumers today fail to make even this limited level of effort - it's simply "too much work" for them. Consider these shortcomings, and it's no wonder that less than 10% of all consumer plastics get recycled. Now, let's see how things get even tougher when we talk about truly reclaiming the plastic materials in their pure form by number.

With plastic reclamation:

- Rinse your plastic bottles repeatedly until there is no trace of the original contents inside. No leftover soft drink, no milk, no soap - nothing.

- If needed, soak the bottles all day or overnight in the sink or bathtub, so all hardened remnants are softened for removal.

- If needed, add food bottles to your regular dishwasher cycle to clean them thoroughly (but only when additional space is available in your normal dishwashing process that would have gone unfilled; we do not advocate wasting water just for the plastics reclamation process.)

- Discard items that would require an inordinate amount of effort or water to clean. If it will require 50 gallons of water and ½ hour of scrubbing to clean a 16-ounce plastic jug, just throw it away; it's not worth the expenditure of your time and labor, and it's not worth consuming that much fresh water to reclaim one plastic jug.

- Meticulously sort all elements of the container. Example: a sports drink bottle. The clear bottle is typically #1 PETE (polyethylene terephthalate) which is perfectly recyclable. The caps and the bottom portion of the ring that is attached to the bottle underneath the mouth are typically made of #5 polypropylene.

- Some bottle caps and rings may contain PVC, which is not easily recycled. Also, the plastic label on the bottle will pollute the pure #1 reclamation process. The label must be removed, the cap must be removed, and the little ring below the cap must be cut off and removed. Only then do you have a pure #1 reclaimable bottle that is ready for shredding and repurposing.

- There will be some plastic packaging products that should

NEVER be recycled; this will require training and ongoing education to monitor.

As you can see, there is a HUGE difference between what people typically think of as 'recycling' and 'reclamation'. WHT is only concerned with **100% pure plastics reclamation**, and there is a definite reason for this. Only "pure" plastic can be used to make the high-quality building materials we will need to build our greenhouses, growing facilities, community buildings, houses, etc. If the plastic materials we start with are mixed and the batches impure, we cannot make high-quality bricks, roof tiles, rebar, windows, frosted side panels, and the other components we need; they will simply not be of the quality needed to make millennium-quality structures. However, if we do it right and keep everything pure - the buildings we construct this year will be still be in use ten or twenty years from now - and potentially a hundred years from now.

Chapter 7 - The Transformation: Converting "Recyclers" into "Reclamation Experts"

So how do we convert recyclers into reclamation experts? The answer is education, hands-on training, and dedication enforced by the acceptance of a clear and concise goal: **solving world hunger**. It will require sacrifice, it will ruffle the feathers of many a well-intentioned recycler, but it will yield a tremendously rewarding end result.

We propose a massive 'education and enlightenment' campaign to bring people up to speed on the importance of the recycling numbers, and the quality control or "QC" that will be necessary for this entire project to work properly. Before we can expect consumers to do a good job in cleaning and sorting their plastics, we have to train them in a way that is clear, understandable, and easy to remember. Therefore, we propose the establishment of two levels of QC among the ranks of WHT.

Plastic Reclamation Sheriff. These are individuals who have completed an advanced training program to learn the intricacies of plastics and plastic sorting. They have attended a trainee promotion seminar, listened to a high-level presentation about the need for quality control in maintaining the integrity of the sort, and completed an extensive Q&A test to prove their knowledge. Sheriffs will be required to pass a series of book tests to prove their knowledge of the entire range of plastics in active use today. They will also be required to pass a manual test in which they must correctly sort a variety of plastic items; this will test their hands-on knowledge of the various plastic components. When the trainee successfully completes all of the training with a 95%+ accuracy rate, they will become a certified Plastic Reclamation Expert or "Sheriff." Their job is to check and verify that everyone is correctly sorting their plastics into the correct bags. They spot-check bags to guard against the mixing of recyclable plastic materials. They will be able to train other consumers in how to sort their household plastics for donation to WHT.

Their counterpart on the consumer side will receive similar training, but in a greatly scaled-down way. We don't want to scare people off, but we DO want them to know the importance of the numerical plastic types -

as well as the importance of NOT recycling things that don't belong in the same group. We anticipate having an online help center, in which people can get the answers they need, any hour of the day or night. For now, a good resource is http://www.plasticsinfo.org.

Plastic Reclamation Guru. These are consumers who have completed the home training course and wish to participate in the plastics reclamation process. In order to become a Guru, you must follow three simple steps:

1. Register on the WHT website. When you do, you will be entered into the system as a plastic reclamation 'candidate' - someone who has raised their hand and indicated a potential interest in learning more about WHT and potentially participating. You will have an online account, protected by a login name and password. This information will stay with you throughout your relationship with WHT.

2. View the online movie. The movie will present the story of plastic recycling, the challenges, the opportunities, etc. - the 'whole enchilada' as they say. The movie will explain why it is so important to separate plastic recyclables by the number - and it will clearly inform the candidate that this will not be an easy process. Many candidates may drop out after viewing the movie - but that's expected; becoming a part of this process will require extreme dedication to detail, and it won't be suited for everybody.

3. Take the online training. A series of training presentations will help candidates learn the basics of the plastic recycling process. After viewing, the candidate must correctly answer a series of questions. They can view the training presentations as many times as needed until they answer the questions correctly. At that point, they move on in their training until completing all steps. Alternative training materials will be available for people without a computer or internet access, or for people who wish to complete the training in a classroom environment.

With such strict training requirements and participation rules, many people will be quick to comment: "Won't that limit the volume of plastic that you are able to collect?" And, in a nutshell, the answer is yes. But the plastic that we DO collect will be 100% pure, and there will little to no sorting effort required after we receive the donations. Our work will be largely complete, because we will have an exceptionally educated and compliant donor base. We believe that the participants in WHT will consider it an honor and a privilege to be participating in this effort, and they will not view their education as having been a waste of time.

Chapter 8 - Putting the Training into Action
Now, You're Ready to Start Reclaiming the Plastic!

After completing the training to become a Sheriff or a Guru, the WHT participant is given a set of bar-coded Photo ID membership cards and key tags, similar to those you receive when signing up for a grocery store's frequent shopper club. The barcode on these cards and tags identifies the participant and the participant's household to the management of WHT (but not to the general public; only WHT will have access to the member database.)

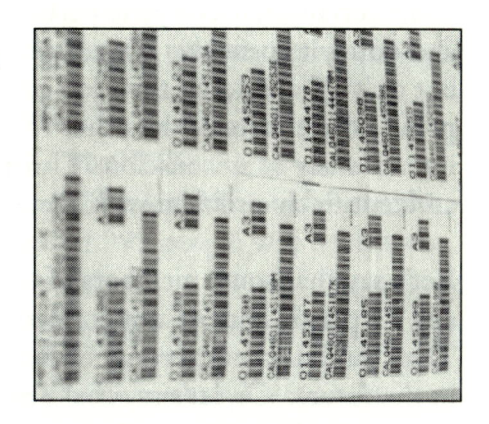

The #1 tool for collecting and storing the reclaimed plastic will be a set of bar-coded / color-coded collection bags. These bags will be consistently color-coded by recycling number, so #1 PETE always goes into white bags, #2 HDPE always goes into green bags, #3, #4 and so forth. A red bag will be used for 'suspect' plastic, i.e. the items that are not marked or cannot be clearly identified as any particular number. This plastic will need to be sorted at a later date by WHT volunteers to determine if it is indeed recyclable.

Batches of these color-coded bags will be available to all participating WHT members at their local collection points - the participating churches, schools, fire departments, community centers, senior centers, etc. who have volunteered to be a weekly, bi-weekly or monthly drop-off point for the local chapter of WHT. When a WHT member picks up a supply of collection bags at their WHT facility, he or she will present their membership card or key tag to be scanned. Next, the barcode on the supply of collection bags will be scanned. The bags are now registered to the individual household and this information is stored in the WHT database.

Privacy Issues: You're Keeping Track of <u>WHAT</u>???

The use of barcodes to track and monitor the member's activity and

39

share the pride that you are performing one of the most vital jobs in our organization.

Be Sure Before You Commit

At the risk of sounding elitist or overbearing, WHT is NOT for everybody. It's going to take work, it's going to require more than a minute or two of your time and it's going to take patience. If your heart is committed but you simply don't have the time or energy to wash your bottles, remove labels, cut off bottle rings, and meticulously sort your plastic, you probably should NOT participate in WHT.

Perhaps you can transfer the responsibility to your children; they may 'buy into' the concept and be willing to do the job after school or on weekends. Or perhaps one of your neighbors is very dedicated and will agree to sort and clean your plastic bottles for you and other people in the neighborhood. For every problem, there is a solution. Be inventive, be creative, and most of all, be cognizant that this will NOT be a quick and easy solution. Nobody wants to make you out to be a bad guy; we simply need 100% good guys on the team if we are to be effective and solve world hunger in our lifetime.

Now That You Have Your Bags Of Reclaimed Plastic, Let's Collect Them!

WHT members will keep color-coded collection bags at home, and fill them during the course of a month. At the end of the month, a collection day will take place at the local WHT collection center. It is important to note that consumers will NOT be allowed to drop off their filled bags any time they wish. We do not want the churches, schools, and fire stations that serve as local WHT participation centers to become garbage dumps! Instead, we propose collecting the bags one day per month - and immediately transferring all of the filled bags to a recycling warehouse that same day.

A typical sorting center will be in the recreation room of the neighborhood church. Sorting will take place on one Saturday morning per month. On that day WHT participants can drop off their bags of impeccably washed, dried and sorted waste plastic containers.

Volunteers at these centers will be trained to identify the correct recycling numbers. These will be the Plastic Reclamation Experts or "Sheriffs" that were mentioned earlier.

As the Plastic Sheriffs come to know their donors, they will know who is reliable and who may require checking. They will mostly spot check the donations to assure that the sort is pure, and make helpful suggestions to those who are making simple mistakes.

These 'plastic sheriffs' will be experts at identifying their specific category of plastic. They will come to know #1 plastic by heart, and be able to recognize properly sorted and cleaned plastic recyclables at a glance. If they find #1 PETE bottles that are properly cleaned but without having the remnant of the cap ring removed, they will demonstrate the proper technique to the donor. They will explain the correct procedures to the consumer, so over time the quality of the plastic separation process will be done in the home and not at the point of recycling.

Some volunteers will pick up bags full of the containers at the homes of senior citizens who cannot get out. Others will have collection routes, where they pick up the bar-coded collection bags from the doorsteps of participating households. As the WHT members become more adept at identifying and sorting their household plastic recyclables, QC will become less of an issue.

If the 'plastic sheriffs' at the WHT collection center encounter items that they are unsure of, they will be able to log into the WHT website and search the database of products by brand name and / or manufacturer, *(see Chapter 34, National Database of Recyclables.)* The WHT online database will feature a master list of brand name products and sizes, and the recycling numbers they carry. "Bogies", i.e. brands that are often packaged in a different number plastic from other brands in the same category, will be listed in the WHT master operating documents. The sorting overseer - the person who is to approve the sorted batches before they are bagged - will be trained to look for these bogies before releasing the batches.

It is our goal to eventually solicit the participation of the manufacturing community. We will contact the various bottlers and packing companies to provide individual product data and photos of each of the containers they manufacture. What better way to prove that you are an environmentally-conscious 'green' company than by announcing to the consumer public that you are a 'treckie' - i.e. **"Total Recycling Compliant"** manufacturer? I.E., every component of your packaging is labeled by plastic type, so each element can be recycled individually. Issuing a PIC (Plastic Identification Code) statement sheet could eventually be as commonplace as issuing a Material Safety Data Sheet (MSDS) that OSHA requires of all chemical manufacturers.

We believe that over time, manufacturers will find that having a 'treckie' logo on their website will become as valuable as displaying a Better Business Bureau seal. As the ranks of WHT membership rise, consumer pressure could eventually drive manufacturers to publish reports identifying the plastic composition of 100% of the elements in their packaging.

And of course, we will constantly be building our database of containers by brand name. As we identify the individual plastic components of specific brand sizes, we will take digital photos and publish the items in our database. By having local chapters contribute to this database, we can quickly build a comprehensive and robust resource for all WHT teams to share.

Ways to Save Storage Space & Reduce Volume

It is important to note that the total amount of space needed to store these items can be reduced 100-fold with a little creativity. Visualize 100 large trash bags full of recyclable plastic. Now visualize the same pile if every yogurt container were stacked together; if every sour cream container were stacked, and every whipped topping container were stacked. You get the idea: the total volume goes down, and the concentration of same-code plastic goes up. You could end up with 500 lbs of recyclable #2 plastic in a small 4' x 4' stack, minimizing the amount

of space needed for storage.
Another issue open for discussion is the question of how to deal with soft drink bottles and milk jugs. They take up a tremendous amount of space, because 99% of their volume is air.

We are hoping that one of the paper-shredding manufacturers can come up with a simple, safe, effective yet affordable machine that will shred these items into plastic strips. Ideally, each recycling center would have two of these machines, one for #1 plastic and one for #2 plastic. They would reduce a mountain of bottles into a bag full of shredded plastic. Since #1 and #2 plastics will make up the lion's share of the plastic that the WHT collection center will take in, the machines will be critical to our long-term success. Here's a golden opportunity for consumer appliance manufacturers and the companies that make paper shredders. This could be your next big product!

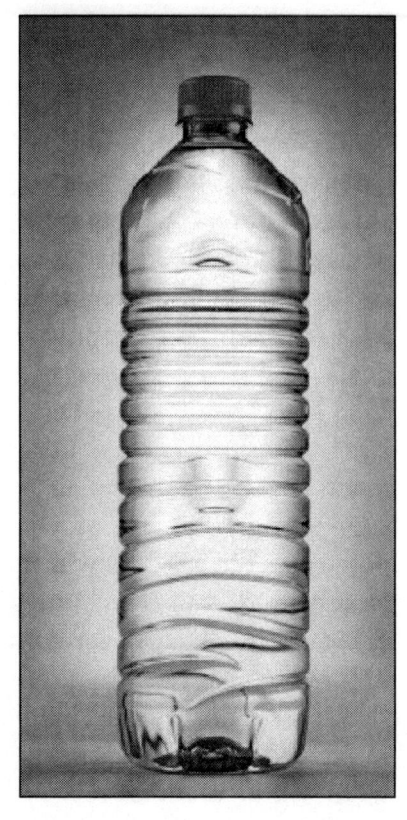

Chapter 9 - Where Does The Plastic Go From Here?

Initially, volunteers will deliver the bags of pure plastic to an empty warehouse collection facility in the largest nearby community. These collected bags will be loaded into semi trailers and taken to a plastic shredding and pelletizing facility. Today, all recycled plastics are melted into solid pellets that look very similar to chunks of chalk or child's play dough. WHT will bag these pellets into large plastic mesh sacks (also made of recycled materials) - similar to a 10 lb. bag of potatoes. These sacks will then be transported to the country or region of final use, where they will be delivered to a factory for conversion into usable building materials.

It is important to note that pelletized recycled plastic is impervious to mold. The sealed bags of plastic pellets will be unbreakable; the outer wrap will be made of recycled plastic as well - similar to the mesh plastic bag that onions are packaged in, but with a much tighter weave so the pellets do not fall out. These sacks of plastic pellets can be shipped under the absolute worst conditions, yet they will sustain little or no physical damage. The pellets are waterproof, mold proof and light weight. Because of their rugged properties, we will be able to ship them very cheaply to all parts of the world.

For example, let's say that a cargo ship has brought a shipment of fresh fruit from Buenos Aires to Miami. Ships like this typically have little or no cargo going back to South America, so they are in essence 'deadheading' - a freight forwarder's term for going back empty-handed. Our sacks of plastic pellets can be loaded into any open area of the ship: the premium storage lockers, into the bilge of the ship, even strapped together on pallets and tied down to the deck. It doesn't matter if the packs are exposed to the rain or wind; it won't damage the material in any way, because it's almost destruction-proof! So we are hoping to enlist the aid of a variety of shipping firms, as well as potentially the U.S. military, to keep our transportation costs low.

What Will Happen to the Plastic Pellets Once They Reach the Destination Country?

The plastic pellets will be delivered to a single conversion plant in the destination country. Here, they will be melted, extruded and or thermoformed into the various building components. The final building products will be trucked to the various installation sites throughout that country. The products will be batched into complete "kits" - i.e., every item needed to build one facility of a specific type. This ready-to-build kit will be shipped by truck, boat, plane, or even freight helicopter, to the designated building site.

Since virtually all of the items in the kit will be made of plastic, the shipment will be able to sustain a high level of abuse without damage, so our freight options are very flexible. Also, because the cost of freight should be relatively inexpensive, we should be able to start with one single conversion plant and serve a large geographic base.

According to industry experts I have spoken with, these plastic conversion plants are available for 'pennies on the dollar' due to the majority of plastics manufacturing moving to China. The clarification I was given by our plastics consultant Steve Gulyas is that there are hundreds of these plants around the world that are currently closed down and collecting dust. He told me that as recently as 2005 many of these plants were being liquidated for 'nickels and dimes' on the dollar, but today they are literally being sold for less than 5% of their original cost. As he put it, "a few years ago you could buy this equipment for a song and a dance. Now, you only need the song."

He told me that in some cases, the owners of the plant might actually donate their machinery to WHT for the tax write-off. Initially, we will start by utilizing existing plastics conversion plants in the destination countries. But as funding increases, it may make sense to purchase existing factories and manage them ourselves, to reduce overhead. What better way to establish a factory to re-manufacture the plastic pellets into building materials than to do it in a plant that is owned and operated by World Hunger Team itself? The operational savings would be phenomenal!

How Will the Recycled Plastic Be Converted into Building Materials?

The beauty of the raw, pure pelletized plastic material is that it is like clay to a sculptor: it can be shaped and molded into just about anything the artist can imagine.

The plastic material, when melted down into its raw liquid form, can be extruded or molded into simple building material components such as:

- **Bricks**. We propose creating hollowed out building blocks - similar to the popular Lego® toy blocks - that can be stacked to create walls. The center of the bricks will be filled with the local soil to add weight.

- **Rebar**. Solid plastic poles will be laced between the blocks, and will also be buried into the earth to act as a foundation.

- **Frosted Side Panels**. Frosted #1 plastic will make ideal translucent side panels. By using two panels per side section, we have a built-in heat buffer. Plus, the trapped chamber can be used as an air duct to circulate air in or out of the building.

- **Window and Door Frames**. #5 Polypropylene plastic should make for ideal, permanent frames that can stand up to heavy use.

- **Doors**. #2 HDPE can make an excellent hollow-frame door.

A wide range of building materials can be made from recycled plastic. It will be up to the plastics experts who join the WHT team, to determine the ideal number of plastic products to use for the various building components.

Who Will Design the Molds?

We have begun initial discussions with another hunger-related group in the Chicago area called **Hands of Love America (HOLA)**, www.handsofloveamerica.org. They are a member of Food for the Hungry International Federation (FHIF), an international relief and development organization to meet the physical and spiritual needs of the poor including emergency relief to those in need, developmental assistance of communities, and educational support to foster the education of children in poverty stricken communities.

My contact at HOLA is very well connected to the business community in Japan, and he has stated that major corporations there may be willing to design and fabricate the molds on a charity basis. Our connection with HOLA and FHIF opens up an entirely new support base and adds an international dimension to our work. The international community is extremely concerned with solving world hunger, and they have significant financial resources to help us expand our service reach very quickly.

Side Note: Metal Recycling

As a side note - and perhaps later in the development cycle of WHT - there will also be a need in our building program for metal items such as screws, hinges, clasps, door knobs, etc. To meet this need, we propose the collection and re-use of metals that are NOT currently being recycled effectively. Good examples are:

- Clothes Hangers
- Candy Tins
- Old Keys
- Old hinges, door knobs / lock assemblies, etc.
- Old plumbing parts such as faucets, pipes, etc.
- Small auto parts such as alternators

How many people actively recycle used metal parts such as these? You just don't think of it! It's easier to throw them into the trash. But what if the local recycling centers added a "small metal parts" bin? It would be easy to collect thousands of pounds of metal in this way. With a little bit of pre-sorting, the smelters could turn this into pure, re-usable metal.

Then, the metal could be turned into usable building components. Metal is actually much easier to recycle than plastics, because of the unique properties of different types of metals.

According to the website www.ehow.com, "once scrap metal is collected and reclaimed, it is often mixed in with other non-metallic materials such as plastic, wood or rubber. In order to sort the metal out from these other materials, the recycled material generally is shredded in a massive industrial shredding machine and then sorted. The sorting process usually involves either magnetic processes or simply sifting processes. At the end of the sorting, the recycling operation is left with a nearly pure form of scrap metal.

"After the scrap metal is sorted, it's entered into a blast furnace that burns at extremely high temperatures. The exact temperature of the furnace varies depending on the metal that is being recycled. The blast furnace melts the scrap metal into its molten (liquid) state and also helps to burn off any impurities or other materials left over from the sorting stage of the process. After the metal is liquefied, it can then be poured into molds for use in new products."

Imagine having access to thousands of tons of recycled metal to make critical items such as cooking grills, pots and pans, tables, chairs, etc. - all of which will be required in the WHT commissaries?

We will also need items such as hinges, screws, nuts and bolts, etc. And again, here is where simplicity has its virtue: by keeping the total number of building components simple and the designs consistent, one hinge could serve a thousand needs. Two or three screw sizes could meet all needs. One door assembly could be used on all doors. "The simpler, the better, " will be the rule of thumb in accessory manufacturing.

Another source of support in this area is to enlist the help of the home do-it-yourself building supply centers. They would jump at the chance to play an active role in a worthy cause such as this. And what better place to get rid of your old faucet assembly once you've replaced it? The advantage to the store: you'll probably drop it off AFTER you've completed your faucet replacement, so it's a trip to the store that you didn't have planned. Retailers love repeat visits, because it typically means repeat purchases.

Yet another view of this issue: why re-invent the wheel? A leading home hardware company would LOVE to be the 'official hardware manufacturer' of WHT. They would use their existing molds and machinery to make the hinges and screws for this project. They'd get a huge tax write-off. And they'd certainly reap the rewards from the PR value they'd receive out of it.

Take note of the difference here: if the U.S. government was the sponsor of this program, a door hinge would cost $50 when all was said and done. However, since a non-affiliated, humanitarian organization is the sponsor of this program, we will certainly find someone to produce the door hinge for free or at their net cost. That is reason #1 for WHT to be totally independent and not affiliated with or owned by any government or for-profit company: we want to stay focused on the end solution of building greenhouses and other growing facilities, at the lowest possible cost. This, in turn, will allow us to feed the greatest number of people at the least possible cost.

Plastic Recycling Summary

The amount of plastic recyclable material that the average family generates in a week is staggering in volume - easily several pounds per week in pure plastic. Harvesting this plastic and keeping it in its pure state by PIC (Plastic Identification Code) will be a daunting task. It will require dedication, consistent action, and plenty of hard work on the part of every WHT volunteer. But just as massive as the task at hand, is the opportunity before us. Each of us has instant, FREE access to the raw materials that can be used to build permanent greenhouses and other structures that will feed and house people in impoverished communities around the world. The sheer power of that statement makes me shiver in anticipation. If you are feeling the same enthusiasm, hang on: we're just getting started.

Chapter 10 - Build Greenhouses

When people think of greenhouses, they probably imagine the little A-frame building behind their grandfather's house where he grew orchids or hothouse tomatoes. That is what greenhouses have traditionally looked like; commercial versions were simply larger structures that had more plant beds across them. They were very humid inside, extremely hot in the summer months, and the temperature was always difficult to regulate.

In our definition, we are using greenhouses as more of a catch phrase; a 'buzz' word, if you will, to make the concept more palatable and understandable to the masses. The building structures we envision are much more diverse and elaborate than greenhouses have ever been before.

Important note: This photo is NOT of a WHT greenhouse, because none exist as of this writing; this photo is of a traditional glasshouse in the Netherlands. WHT is in its start-up phase and we are just now soliciting the involvement of architects and engineers to create our greenhouse designs.

Before we discuss the actual design and construction of these greenhouses, let's ask an obvious but necessary question:

Why build greenhouses?

It may seem like a trivial question, but it's actually a very good one. The truth is, in a perfect world, every nation would have thousands if not millions of acres of productive farmland growing mass quantities of food. The farmers would be experts in their craft and could overcome any challenges that are thrown at them, man-made or natural.

Distribution channels would be in place to deliver the freshly harvested food to people across the nation. And the people of the nation would be fully employed and could pay a fair price for the farmer's products. This was the game plan for many years, and one that many countries still follow. But what happens when one or more of these conditions are not in place? The truth is, any one shortfall can upset this entire food chain, and the people on the receiving end are the ones who suffer most of all: in short, they just don't get enough food.

Greenhouses, however, as well as hothouses (simple covered and protected growing plats) are controllable food production factories. If properly managed, these facilities can maintain the ideal growing conditions for a multitude of different fruits and vegetables. Among all of these facility types, greenhouses provide the maximum in control (as well as the maximum in complex maintenance.) Whatever the outside conditions, whatever the temperature or humidity or rainfall levels, the conditions inside a greenhouse can be regulated to assure that the plants have everything they need to produce edible food at the maximum yield. It's a sure thing, and there aren't too many sure things in some parts of the world today.

Why Not Just Build More Conventional Farms?

It is important to note that while greenhouses can produce **micro** amounts of food, traditional farms can produce **macro** amounts of food - and ideally all of the world's food production needs could be handled on a **macro** level. But that hasn't proven effective in many countries. The soil is too overworked, there is not enough rainfall or local water for irrigation, the financing is not present to purchase seed or tools or fertilizer, or the knowledge needed to overcome the environmental challenges, or the tools for communicating that knowledge are just not there. There are technology issues, language issues, transportation issues, funding issues - the list goes on and on. The reality is that dozens of challenges are present, any one of which can hinder local farmers from effectively doing their jobs.

With that said, let's take note of an important truth: Greenhouses cannot replace farmers. Can we ever build enough greenhouses to completely replace farmers or the mass-production of food? Hardly. But greenhouses and similar growing facilities CAN be effective in providing some level of sustenance in the most food-challenged parts of the world.

Why Not Just Improve The Existing Farms?

It is one thing to develop grandiose plans to change the farming conditions in these developmentally challenged countries. It is quite another thing to actually construct massive irrigation projects to sustain large-scale farms, to airlift in the massive supplies and countless tons of equipment that will be needed, and to train the existing farmers in modern farming techniques. That is why most charities simply airlift in thousands of pounds of ready-to-eat food to starving nations; it doesn't require as much capital commitment. This approach works, and it definitely needs to continue so the nutritional needs of people in these starving nations can be met. But this is not a total solution.

There will be days - weeks - even months during which the delivery of food will be impossible due to funding shortfalls, shortage of food supplies, logistical snags, etc. Meanwhile, there is a lineup of several million people knocking at the door. They need sustenance. They don't want to hear that "help will be here soon" or that "within a few years" we can make major changes in the farming situation. That is all 'nice to know', but their concern is today. They need food in their belly today, or they may die tomorrow.

The starving nations of the world need the quickest possible help that can be provided, and they're not going to be too fussy about who provides it or how. So before anyone debates the merits of small-scale food production vs. large-scale production, please answer one question: what are you going to serve them for lunch, today? How about tomorrow, and the next day, and the next day? Let's talk menu, and let's talk deliverables. Can you be there every day, every week, and every year from now on? A local food production facility *can* be. It can provide a sustainable source of food - however small - to provide at least the bare nutritional essentials required for continued life.

As the plans presented in this book demonstrate, we can build **hundreds and thousands** of greenhouses for very little cash - largely using waste materials that are currently being discarded. And once they are built and functioning, the charitable organization and the skilled people who built them can leave; the native residents can operate them and the local community can support themselves, for many years to come.

It's easy to downplay this concept as being too little, too late. You could look at the total output of one greenhouse for one day and realize that it "only" produced 20 lbs of tomatoes. "Hardly enough to bother with," the experts might say. But the greenhouse next door to it might have produced 50 lbs of green beans. And the one next to that might have produced 30 lbs of squash.

So with as few as three greenhouses operating in one community, you have 100 lbs of food to serve that day. Granted, it's not the 5,000 lbs of food you would want to be available there every day. But it's enough food to provide a full day's nutrition to about 200 people. Or it could be enough food to provide starvation avoidance and minimal sustenance to about 500 people. And it will keep producing food year round.

The simple greenhouses in which this food will be grown, will be constructed from trash: the plastic discards of about one week's consumption in a typical city of 10,000 people here in the U.S. So we could easily produce 1,000 greenhouses over the course of a few short years, yielding 100,000 lbs of food per day in a country that now has little to no food.

SIDE NOTE TO THE 'EXPERTS': When downplaying or 'pooh-poohing' this idea as being an ineffective solution to world hunger, please submit your alternative solution to this litmus test:

- **COST**: must use 'free' or 'almost free' materials.
- **IMPLEMENTATION**: must not require utility-supplied electricity or running water.
- **CONSTRUCTION**: must be simple to construct by minimally-trained workers.
- **STABILITY**: Facilities must be semi-permanent, and require little to no maintenance, ever.
- **OPERATION**: must use local, unskilled talent to operate.
- **OUTPUT**: must provide a steady output of edible, wholesome food, each and every day.
- **RE-STOCKING**: must need little or no outside support or purchased supplies to operate effectively.
- **HANDS-OFF**: once you build your solution, you must leave and almost never come back. The locals prefer it that way.

Any takers, experts? We're waiting on your call...

Chapter 11 - Mankind Needs Buildings of All Types

Hunger is just one problem facing the world's impoverished masses; there are many others. Human beings have other needs besides eating. Of course, food is the primary requirement in life. But there are other needs in the communities we will serve, and we believe that our concept of using recycled plastics as building materials has further merit in solving other problems in the needy communities of the world, specifically:

a. **Housing**. Permanent homes can be made of recycled plastic.
b. **Medical Facilities.** Semi-permanent shelters can be installed quickly and cheaply, with fine mesh screens that prevent mosquito bites and the spread of malaria.
c. **Water Purification**. Water collection facilities can be built of recycled plastic, with built-in solar heating systems that boil and purify the water.
d. **Community Buildings**. Local government can thrive when office facilities are available to house and store public records.
e. **Education and Culture**. Permanent schoolhouses, sports facilities - even theaters can be built out of recycled plastics.
f. **Commercial Buildings**. Local economies can grow when businesses have facilities to operate out of.

Why Do the Impoverished Areas of the World Need More Buildings?

The greatest need for more buildings is not in the major industrialized countries; we have new houses and shopping malls popping up like mushrooms every day. There is plenty of capitalization in our neck of the woods. But how much development is taking place in the remote parts of Africa, South America, Haiti, Mexico, and countless other countries? Why aren't Wal-Mart®, Taco Bell®, and TGI Friday's® dropping huge structures into these outlying areas? There are certainly plenty of people living there; plenty of need for new clothes, lots of hungry mouths to feed. All they're missing is one key factor: **money**. There IS LITTLE TO NO CAPITAL at play in the outlying corners of the earth. And guess what, folks? The outlying areas outnumber the prosperous areas 100 to 1!

The last major effort to build new structures in outlying areas came in the 1930s as part of the Work Projects Administration, (WPA;

affectionately known as "We Piddle Around.") The WPA built park buildings, community structures, museums, homes, city halls - you name it, they built it.

Many of the Mexican Americans living in the U.S. participated in WPA projects. When the WPA program was ending, some of these people - even those who were legalized Americans - were 'repatriated' back to Mexico, and they took their WPA knowledge with them. They built community buildings and homes in the poorest parts of Mexico during the 1930's.

I recently saw a documentary on current political upheaval in the remote parts of Mexico. The filmmaker was interviewing people with little or no capital or resources, and asking them how they were going to vote. These people were living in huts - they had no money and were barely eking an existence out of the undeveloped land. And where did they congregate to be filmed? They gathered in front of a dilapidated 1930's WPA-style building; a building with no windows, no door, a building that was obviously rotted and in need of massive renovation. But it was the only structure in town, so it had become the community center! Imagine that - no new buildings were erected in the area for more than 70 years due to lack of funding, materials or knowledge - the three elements that the concerted effort of the WPA brought together to become the mindset of the day!

The World Needs New Buildings

Buildings provide protection from the elements. Just as peas need their pod to grow, people need buildings to keep out the wind / rain / heat / cold at different times of the year. The more diverse the range of buildings in a community, the greater the community's ability to house, feed, protect and nurture its people. When a community has buildings for the various needs of life - living, learning, sharing, relaxing - the process of life can continue unabated. By removing the obstacles of finding shelter and nutrition, we are opening new avenues for the community to become healthy and thriving.

The unique thing about World Hunger Team is that we are not asking for billions of dollars to build conventional structures; we are proposing to build these structures out of everyday household trash. Over 90% of post consumer plastic is currently benefiting nobody. To the contrary, these non-biodegradable plastics are hurting our environment and clogging our landfills, oceans and streams. Wouldn't it be better to put these materials to good use and build a more vibrant society in the neediest parts of the world? If you follow this chain of thinking, you "get" the big idea behind WHT.

Why Not Just Build Conventional Structures?

The primary differences between conventional development and our proposed method of development are:

- **Cost**. By using donated plastic as the primary component of the building materials, we dramatically reduce construction cost.

- **Simplicity**. Our construction plans will be very simple in nature, allowing unskilled workers to assist in building the facilities with minimal supervision.

- **Permanence**. The beauty of building with plastic is that it is water-resistant, it does not need paint, and it will not rot. It IS, however, subject to UV degredation, as discussed in Chapter 20.

The downside of using plastic in building construction is that it does not 'breathe' - i.e. there is no air flow inherent in the structure itself. This will be a challenge that the engineers must address in every single structure that is designed.

Another downside condition is that plastic will sweat - i.e. collect condensation from the environment and the inhabitants. This also must be addressed by the engineers.

Why Not Build State-of-The-Art Structures Instead of Simple Buildings?

There will be some voices raised proclaiming that 'only the best' should be used when meeting the needs of the poor. Why have one standard of building quality for the well-to-do, while building primitive structures for the less fortunate? This philosophy is one huge reason among many as to why the poor of the world have so little today. If we wait until that 'golden day' when the world can afford to build high-tech homes, schools, farms and community buildings in the far-reaching corners of the earth, that day may never come.

Think of it this way: it typically costs well over one million dollars to build a single health clinic in a suburban American city. It will serve the community well and provide excellent services from its opening day. In a remote corner of Africa, the need exists for this very same facility - and the need is probably far greater in that community than in the U.S. city, due to lack of competition.

The difference between the two needs is that the U.S. clinic's builders can typically obtain the million dollars through conventional financing. There will be paying customers who will provide capital to repay the loan. But with the clinic in Africa, the million dollars in capital is simply not there.

Even if funding could be obtained, the parents of the sick children who would be treated in the clinic could not pay, so there would be no return on investment to the financier. The costs would continue to roll in, however, for everything from medicine to bandages, from test equipment to paper supplies. In many cases, the only way the million dollars can be raised is through charity donations - and giving is way down in our current worldwide recession. Because there is no funding for such an advanced building, no building of any type is built or available to the citizens of the community. The need goes unmet, and the people in the poor African village continue to die from simple, treatable ailments.

Let's suppose that the people of the African community save their pennies and nickels over a 20-year period to help finance the clinic. What is to become of the people who need treatment during those 20 years? Should they go on being sick and dying, because they deserve "only the best" and not settle for an interim solution?

The bottom line is that _good enough is often all that is needed_. Sometimes, meeting your short-term needs is more important than satisfying your long-term goals or grandiose self-image.

If you are totally opposed to using simple structures to help meet the day-to-day needs of the world's neediest people, do something about it: go out and raise the million dollars needed to build a state-of-the-art clinic in that remote African village. And when you've built it, stay out on the road raising funds, because the bills will be arriving weekly. And remember that you've only solved that community's _health_ needs. What about their _food_ needs, their _housing_ needs, their _educational_ needs, their _government_ needs, their _social_ needs, etc., etc., etc.? And you've 'only' helped _one_ small community in _one_ small corner of Africa. There are **tens of thousands of other communities** around the world who have the same needs. How are you going to raise the funds to meet all of _their_ needs?

Clinics, schools and homes in the poorest regions of the world are often poorly constructed and in need of major repairs. They often provide very little protection from the elements.

The fact is, good intentions are wonderful things to embrace, but life requires action. As the late, great Ray Charles said when asked about his keys to success, he replied, "It's not what I think, what I say or know, it's what I _do_."

In solving any problem, it's what you DO that makes the difference. The WHT solution can be DONE, because it harnesses the combined wisdom and talents of many, and because it does not rely on massive funding from already-stressed charitable foundations. It uses building materials that are largely free. Yes, there will be expense incurred to collect, store, recycle, transport, and reconstrude the plastic - but these costs will be a fraction of the cost of using conventional building materials purchased on the open market.

Our approach may be considered too primitive by some, but bear in mind that the poor communities we will be serving have little to nothing now. Our approach will be advanced technology compared to the way they are doing things now.

Bringing Advanced Technology to Play in Simplified Building Structures

The important items to bear in mind when creating and implementing a new building system on this scale are:

    a. **The materials and building concepts may be new, but the construction methodology is not.** The human race has been building structures for thousands of years. Our goal is not to replace conventional building engineering and construction knowledge, but to learn from it, harness all of the expertise that exists today, and add to it. Bear in mind that the experts who will be developing the building plans and construction techniques that WHT implements will not be amateurs or unskilled neophytes; we hope to enlist the largest contracting engineer firms, architects, developers and contractors in the world as part of WHT.

    b. **"Good" can often be better than "best" if the greater need is served.** It would be nice to say that every facility we install can be a permanent solution to the problem, and that we will always utilize the best and highest technology available today. But if we can rapidly implement 100 structures that are "acceptable" vs. one facility that is the "best" solution, we will achieve a much higher success rate at a lower overall cost.

    c. **K.I.S.S.** The polite explanation of this is "keep it simple and sincere." In our maiden voyage, we must develop quick and simple plans that are easily implemented and replicated. As the team of members grows and we continue to receive input from the people using the facilities, we will refine the building plans to make improvements. Enhancements and refinements will be ongoing from day one, but the critical thing is to start with our best knowledge today and begin taking action.

Chapter 12 - WHT Expanded Role: Housing

When a major disaster strikes, like the typhoon in Myanmar (Burma) or the earthquake in China, hundreds of thousands of people are without shelter. It could potentially take years to replace the houses that were destroyed.

As the photo at right shows, many of the existing homes in poor countries are little more than shacks that cannot stand up to the strong winds of a typhoon. So when a storm hits, the entire population can literally become homeless overnight.

WHT proposes a solution that is more than temporary, but shy of permanent: thermoformed (vacuum formed) tents made from huge sheets of recycled #2 plastic. Here's how this concept works:

A giant thermoforming mold is created, in the shape of a domed family-sized tent, i.e. 8 feet wide, 8 feet deep, 6 feet high at the edges and 8 feet high at the peak.

A large sheet of recycled #2 plastic is used to create the tent. The thickness of the plastic is considerably thicker than a milk jug, giving the finished tent strength and resistance to crushing. In the thermoforming process, the sheet of plastic is clamped into a rigid frame and then heated in a dual-sided oven that resembles a giant toaster oven.

When the plastic is sufficiently pliable, the frame is quickly moved over the thermoforming mold and locked into place. A vacuum pump below the mold is turned on, in essence sucking the wind out of the hollow space between the plastic sheet and the mold. The pliant plastic sheet is drawn down and conforms to the shape of the mold. When cooled, the resulting product is in essence a giant hard-plastic tent.

Several locations in the mold feature ridges that indicate the location of openings that will be cut out after completion of the molding process:

• A round opening at the top, approximately 1' in circumference. This is the air vent, much like the opening at the top of a native American teepee. A rain cap will be added above this opening, installed on location.

• A door opening in the front, about 2-1/2 feet wide by 4' high, starting approximately 1 foot off the ground.

• A sliding combination window screen / door assembly will be created separately and affixed to the front of the tent using a solvent that will weld the door frame to the tent. The screen can be closed independently of the solid plastic door, allowing air filtration during the day while keeping insects out.

• One window opening on both the left and right sides, approximately 1" square. A window screen will be permanently affixed to the outside of tent using solvent. A plastic outer flap will be affixed above the window frame, and Velcro fasteners will be added above and below the window panel. This will allow the outer flap to be secured down over the window frame preventing rain water and light from entering the tent, or raised and secured up above the window frame, allowing the free passage of light and air through the window during the day.

A simple ice cube tray is an excellent example of thermoforming. A sheet of thin plastic is heated to make it pliable, and then the flexible plastic is sucked into a mold to give it the desired shape. We can make temporary homes using this same process.

• An excess lip of plastic is left around the edge of the tent. Holes will be melted into the corners and middle panels of the edges, and large 1 foot plastic tent stakes will be used to anchor the tent to the ground during installation. Two holes will be placed on the front, one to either side of the door opening, to prevent occupants from tripping on the spikes during entry or exit from the tent.

A tent base is also thermoformed out of a sheet of recycled #2 plastic. The base matches the outer dimensions of the tent, i.e. 8' x 8', but the base is only 1' deep. Visualize the bottom of a milk jug that is cut at the 1" mark. This base is the key to keeping water and insects out of the tent. In the four corners of this base, excess plastic flaps are left in place, and holes are melted into the four corners.

When the base is placed in location on-site, a rope is used to draw the edges of this base inward. The tent 'dome' is lowered into place above the base. The installer enters the tent, applies solvent around the edges of the base, and then releases the ropes. The edges of the base open up to align with the interior edges of the dome, and additional solvent is applied to the edges, melting the two units into a permanent sealed unit.

Because the door opening is 1 foot off the ground, the tent will now remain dry inside during the rain, and run off water will not enter the tent unless it exceeds 11" in depth.

The reason for this two-step process is simple: logistics. Multiple units of the bottomless dome portion of the tent unit can be stacked together for shipment. A rope can be extended through the center of the domes and hooked to a bundle of the tent bottoms, held together through the plastic flaps. In essence, a stack of 30 or more of these two-part units can be held together for transit, much like CDs stacked on a pole. A military helicopter could deliver a huge stack of these tents to a remote location in a single trip.

This is just one idea to provide a temporary solution to housing relief in the most destitute regions of the world. Addressing the permanent needs of these communities will be a key factor in the advanced challenges facing the World Hunger Team.

WHT Expanded Role: Schools and Community Resource Buildings

Another huge need in impoverished areas is the lack of community buildings, i.e. schools, government offices, recreational facilities, etc. Permanent buildings are needed, yet budget dollars and construction materials are often in short supply. The African school (masai) shown below is typical of the state of community buildings in poor areas. Imagine your child attending school in this building during monsoon season!

One company that has taken on the challenge of creating quality structures in low-income areas is **Sahara Technologies** of Sao Paulo, Brazil. It has developed a unique method of making bricks out of a mixture of local soil and cement known as 'Olaria Ecologica' (ecological brickworks). It uses soil-cement and soil-lime-cement processes which negate the need to bake the bricks.

According to their website, www.sahara.com.br/en1.html, "this means a zero impact on the ecosystem both in terms of deforestation or smoke particles from the baking process." The bricks are actually manufactured on site using a portable hand-operated machine (see below) that presses the bricks out of a mixture of local soil and cement. The brick design allows them to be interlocked, much like Lego® pieces, and the two internal cavities allow the use of rebar as well as running pipes and electrical conduits through the building's outer walls. The bricks are held together using a thin layer of soil/cement mixture. The company claims that 3 laborers can make 150-200 bricks per hour, and that 1,000 bricks can be made using 2,500 litres of soil and only 6 sacks of cement.

We believe there is significant merit in utilizing this remarkable brickmaking process in conjunction with building components made of recycled plastic. The net result will be permanent buildings that will be extremely economical to produce as well as elegant and long-lasting.

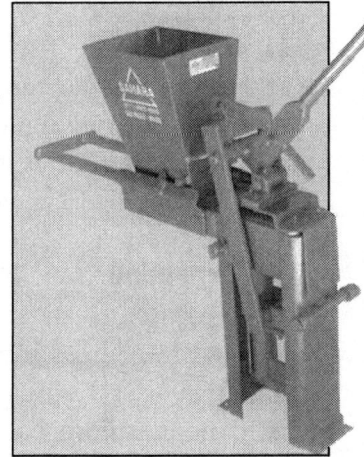

Photos © Sahara Tecnologia, Màquinas E Equipamentos LTDA.

Chapter 13 - Current Conditions and Resources in Target Communities

In many of the communities and villages that this program will serve, little to no resources are currently available. When hunger relief workers arrive in a remote village, they will typically find:

- Little to no organized agricultural production
- What few gardens exist are subject to failure based on:
  - Shortage of rainfall
  - Poor growth due to lack of fertilizer and / or weak soil conditions
- Vandalism by hungry neighbors or animals
  - Shortage of tools to till the soil or weed the crops
  - Lack of seeds
  - Gardens are subject to sun / frost and / or weather damage
  - In addition, no support buildings are present to house the farming equipment or raise seedlings in a protected environment.
  - Living conditions are often poor; what few structures exist can often lack doors or windows, and roofs can be leaky. Little money is available to make repairs, and building supplies are typically not available locally.

The needs of these villages are massive; they need significant influx of capital, expertise, manpower and supplies to rectify the situation. The churches, social groups and charities are making inroads, but they can only do so much.

These conditions are prevalent in the majority of the world's countries, not just in a few isolated areas. So how can a relief organization find the resources to change the world - especially when they are using conventional resources and funding? The reality is that without a huge change in the mindset and commitment of the world's wealthy, there are not going to be sweeping changes in the living conditions for the worlds' poor.

BUT - with the WHT concept, we hope to change several key components of the solution:

- **COST.** We will be using 'free' materials; waste products that people will gladly donate.

- **EXPERTISE.** We will be centralizing the expertise needed to construct the facilities, using the internet to bring together highly-skilled professionals in dozens or even hundreds of niche disciplines from around the world.

- **SIMPLIFICATION.** We are removing the need for expert construction staff in remote locations. The engineering advantages and construction efficiencies will be pre-designed into each structure.

- **PRE-ENGINEERED FOR THE SPECIFIC CONDITIONS OF THE INSTALLATION SITE.** We are pre-engineering the designs of the buildings to function effectively in the specific temperature / humidity conditions of the installation site. The temperature control systems will be radically different in each of five different climate brackets:
    - Hyper-Arid
    - Arid
    - Semi-Arid
    - Sub-Humid
    - Humid

    An excellent source of information on the specific conditions of countries around the world can be found at the website of the Food and Agriculture Organization of the United Nations, http://www.fao.org

- **SUPPORT.** We are significantly minimizing the amount of financial, material and manpower support needed after implementation.

Chapter 14 - The WHT Building Concepts

We believe that there will be a need for two basic types of growing facilities in the WHT installations: **Micro** (small-scale growing) and **Macro** (large-scale growing).

Micro facilities will be enclosed or semi-enclosed buildings offering protection from the environment.

Macro facilities will be non-enclosed farming plats with irrigation support.

The **Micro** facilities will provide a 'quick fix' and provide some daily sustenance to the local community. These facilities can be built rapidly and start producing food in mere weeks after implementation. Where people are dying of malnutrition, we need to deliver food in the quickest-possible time-frame.

The **Macro** facilities will provide long-term gains to the greater food production needs of the overall area. These facilities will likely be joint ventures with the commercial farmers in the area.

Two Types of Micro Buildings

Two types of small-scale buildings will be needed:

1. Full-Protection / Sealed Greenhouses (true greenhouses.) These are temperature-controlled, moisture-controlled buildings for year-round food production.

2. Limited-Protection Growing Facilities (hothouses.) These will be permanent structures with limited environmental controls. In essence, they are semi-protected growing beds with built-in irrigation sprayers. The sides of the structures consist of fencing with heavy strip plastic interwoven into the fencing. The sides provide limited protection from wind damage and intruders.

The advantage to these structures is that they can be produced for a fraction of the cost of the full-protection greenhouses. This will allow us to build 10 or more of these structures for the same cost and time investment of a full-protection greenhouse. These facilities will be dormant in the winter months.

The local conditions will determine what types of micro buildings are needed at a WHT facility. If the conditions are very harsh, only full-protection buildings will be installed. If the conditions are not as harsh, both types of micro buildings will be installed.

Principals of Construction

We propose the development of five primary exterior building materials:

a. Building Blocks. Create hollow blocks out of recycled type #2 HDPE (High Density Polyethylene) plastic. The blocks are glued together with solvent to form a row. The hollow areas are filled with local dirt to add weight and substance. The next layer of blocks seals the dirt in, forming a permanent wall. The middle, edges, and sides of the blocks feature indentations and holes to merge with the rebar.

> *(NOTE: dyed #1 PETE will be sorted by color, so green 'lemon-lime' drink bottles will be used to create green bricks, yellow 'skim milk' bottles will be used to create yellow bricks, etc.)*

b. Frosted Side Panels. Create light-transmitting frosted light panels out of #2 HDPE - specifically frosted milk jugs. These panels will be in essence large light panels. They will be interspersed between the structural building-block posts, and they will be double-paned with an air channel between them to buffer the exterior temperature.

c. Corner Sections. These are primarily for cosmetic purposes, but they will also add strength & support.

d. Rebar. Create rebar out of #5 PP Polypropylene plastic, *(bottle caps, ketchup bottles, yogurt containers and margarine tubs, medicine bottles.)* The rebar will be run vertically and horizontally between the blocks, extending four feet into the ground, to add strength and wind resistance to the structures.

e. Roofing Panels. These will be made out of clear #1 PETE, so light can pass through them to the plants below - but water stays out.

Here is a very rough sketch of how this building might look upon completion:

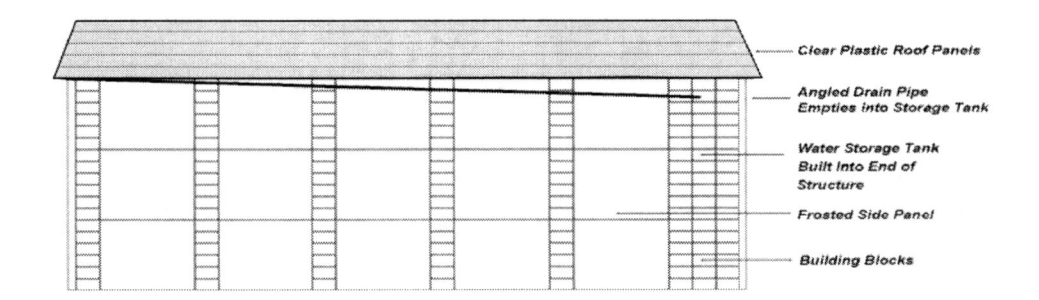

- Clear Plastic Roof Panels
- Angled Drain Pipe Empties into Storage Tank
- Water Storage Tank Built Into End of Structure
- Frosted Side Panel
- Building Blocks

DISCLAIMER: *Please note that this is a laymen's sketch of the core building components; the actual building plans will be drawn by a trained architect to assure that engineering rules are maintained and proper weight & stress controls are followed. Also note that this sketch does not show the entryway, which is discussed in Chapter 17.*

It is important to note that WHT is in its START-UP PHASE. As such,

- NO buildings have been constructed to date.
- These designs have NOT been tested for functionality, nor have they been reviewed or approved by a building engineer or architect.

The entire concept of WHT is in its FORMATIVE STAGE. We are soliciting the help of professionals in ALL facets of building design and construction to help us make this dream a reality. So, professional engineers and architects, before you jot off a note to me starting with the words, "Dear Moron", please know that I will simply contact you right back asking you to volunteer to redo these designs correctly.

- *Have a better way of doing things? Tell us.*
- *Have a better design or approach to solving a problem? Jot it down and send it in.*

That being said, let's look at some VERY ELEMENTARY concepts in building design and methodology. And if you are a building contractor, engineer or architect - or if you are an expert in materials manufacturing, please 'tell it like it is'. Nothing about WHT is locked in stone, especially when it comes to technical issues. YOU are the expert, we are simply the typical client who knows what they want to accomplish but hasn't got a clue about what it's going to take to actually build it...

Construction Methodology

The basic premise of our building construction design features an innovative use of rebar to add strength and permanence to the building.

- Create rebar in 4' and 8' lengths
- Rebar is used two different ways:
  a. As traditional cross-bracing to add support to the walls
  b. As anchor posts into the ground

The purpose of the anchor posts is to give the building permanence and stability against wind, impact, flood waters, etc.

- Post holes are dug into the ground at key points along the building perimeter. Anchor wings (similar to propeller blades) are attached to an 8' section of rebar and locked into place with solvent.

- The 8' winged rebar is placed into the post hole and fed through the first layer of brick. Approximately 4' of the rebar is above ground, the balance is below ground.

- Once the above-ground rebar posts are level at a 4' height, the post holes are filled with a concrete-like substance to permanently secure the post in place. We propose the development of a concrete substitute made of solvent-melted plastic and local dirt. The materials will be easier than concrete to transport to remote locations, plus the material will not break down over time. In theory, this plasticized concrete should be impervious to breakdown from water seepage, rot, or bugs.

- Once the first four layers of interlocking bricks are put in place, additional rebar is cross-woven into the bricks down to the 2' level. In other words, middle holes in the brick that do not have rebar will now receive it, adding additional reinforcement to the design.

- Caps will be fused to the bottom hole at the 2' level, using solvent. This will hold the rebar in place while the additional levels are added.

The building blocks will also provide strength, stability, weight and substance to the building.

- The bricks will be designed with four large open valleys (see illustration on next page.)

- The hollow bricks will be firmly sealed in place, using solvent to fuse the edges to the surrounding bricks and to the rebar.

- Once the layer is effectively fused in place, the valleys in the brick will be filled with local dirt and/or rocks.

- Once the valleys are full, the next layer is added.

- The top row of bricks will be capped off with sealing panels that fit snugly into the valleys. This will prevent water from seeping into the exposed areas and harboring bugs, algae, or rot.

- The roof foundation will be attached to the building using rebar that extends just beyond the top of the final row of bricks. This foundation will be made of rebar, and locked in place using 3-pronged peak caps (wide angle) and 3-pronged edge caps (tight angle).

- The caps are designed to fit into the open holes in the bricks. They are fused into place at the appropriate locations.

- The roof foundation is built on the roof top using rebar that is fused into position into the open holes of the edge caps and peak caps.

The roof will be one of the most critical components of the building, as it will be exposed to the greatest amount of weather abuse and damaging UV (ultra violet) light exposure.

- Once the rebar roof foundation is complete, plastic roofing sections will be fused to the foundation using solvent.

- The bottom row is affixed first, with the edge leading into gutter channels that are fused to the edge of the wall. These gutters angle down the side of the building and lead into a water storage tank that is built into the side of the building.

- Roof layers are added up to the roof peak.

- The peak receives special peak-cap panels that are v-shaped; this forces rainwater down the rooftop, into the gutters, and into the water storage tank.

- When the water tank is full, floating caps will seal the tank and additional rainwater will bypass the tank and flow into traditional downspouts.

Building Block - Top View

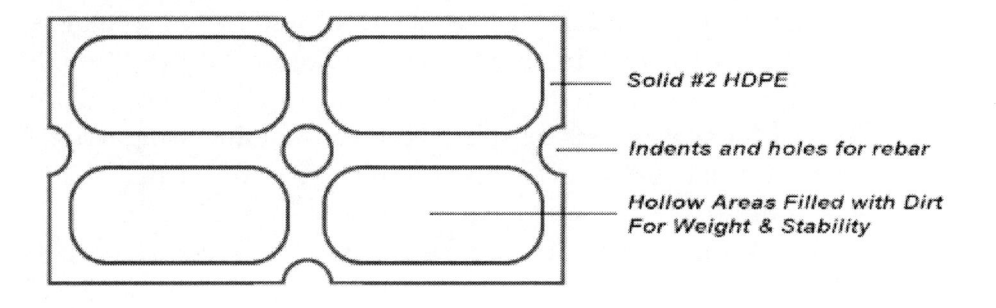

Solid #2 HDPE

Indents and holes for rebar

Hollow Areas Filled with Dirt For Weight & Stability

Building Block - End View

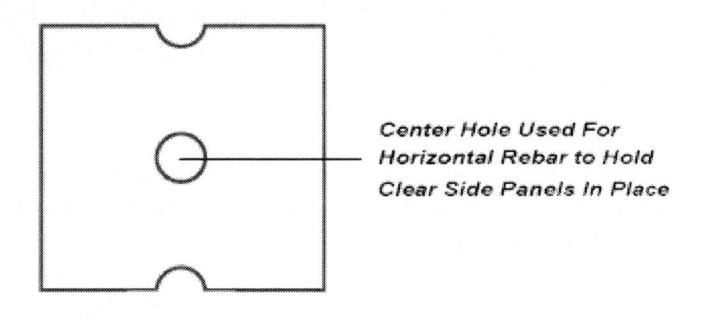

Center Hole Used For Horizontal Rebar to Hold Clear Side Panels In Place

Frosted Panel Holder - Top View

— Indents Hold Clear Panels In Place

— Circular Nodule Connects To Notch in Brick

Rebar - Side View

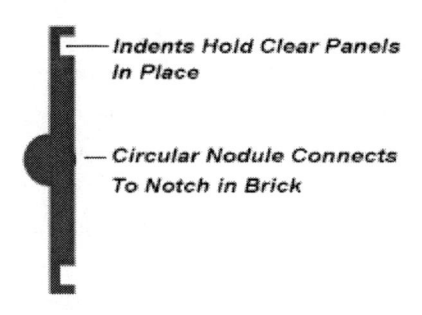

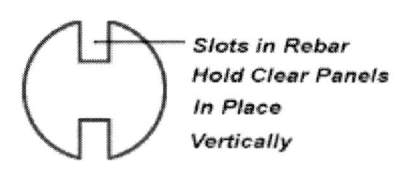

— Slots in Rebar Hold Clear Panels In Place Vertically

Corner Section - Top View

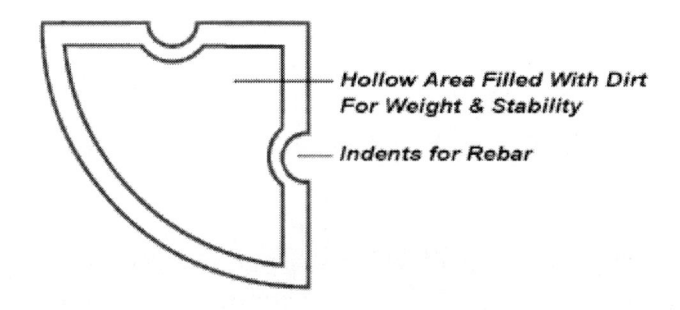

— Hollow Area Filled With Dirt For Weight & Stability

— Indents for Rebar

As you may have noticed in the rough drawings shown above, all of the elements of this building are kept extremely simple, yet some fundamentally strong features are maintained:

• Rebar is used throughout the structure to add strength. When the connecting points are coated with solvent at time of assembly, the two surfaces will fuse into one, providing permanent strength and adhesion. In the world of plastics, solvent does not act like glue. Rather, it liquifies the core elements of the plastic on both surfaces. The molecular strands co-mingle in this liquified 'soup' and the two surfaces become one. If the two surfaces are sufficiently liquified, they literally become one and cannot separate back into their original form. In other words, they're not going to be coming apart in the future - regardless of the duress that they receive. When you are constructing buildings that you hope will last a long time, this is a very good thing.

• This same rebar is implemented across the structure and is used to support the growing beds. Additional rebar is used vertically to transfer the weight of the growing beds down to the ground.

• A water storage tank is built into the end of the building. This section will be extremely well enforced with rebar and large retaining caps to hold in the tremendous weight of the stored water. The interior chamber will be sprayed with molten plastic several times to assure a waterproof seal. The concept here is to collect massive amounts of water during the monsoon season, and use it to water the plants during the dry season.

• An angled drain pipe will be installed on both sides of the roof to collect the water and divert it into the storage tank.

• The vertical columns of building blocks provide column strength to the building.

• The frosted side panels allow significant light distribution throughout the building.

• The roof panels also allow light filtration into the building. The actual transparency of these panels will vary by region; a major issue in greenhouses is often TOO MUCH sunlight and heat.

Chapter 15 - Controlling Temperatures Within the Greenhouses

Perhaps the largest factor in maintaining ideal growing conditions within the greenhouse will be temperature. In conventional greenhouses, a complex array of heaters and air conditioners is needed to keep temperatures from hitting extremes.

Traditional HVAC Methods Not Practical

A heat pump system would provide the ideal levels of heat transfer, but there are implementation issues to consider. The primary problem is location: many of these growing facilities will be located in very remote regions of the earth, where there is no local electricity or water supply. Plus, there is the cost factor to consider; there will be little money to construct and / or maintain these facilities. Also, there will be scant availability of trained repair personnel to maintain and repair the heat pump equipment. What is needed is a low power-consumption, simple heat exchange system that can function for many, many years with little to no maintenance. Simple lubrication and replacement of bearings and motors is feasible, but complex technical repairs will not be easily implemented and therefore complex equipment must be avoided.

Different Cooling Methods for Different Climates

In areas of moderate temperature, we propose using 'cave effect' air transfer. In areas of extreme dry heat, we propose using traditional evaporative / wet air coolers, lovingly known as 'swamp coolers'.

The "Cave Effect" - Using Geothermal Heat Exchange to Maintain Greenhouse Temperature

Where temperatures are moderate, we propose tapping into the natural 'cave effect' found in the underground soil. We've all heard about arctic explorers who have dug holes in the ground to escape the bitter outdoor temperatures. The same concept applies in very hot environments. The temperature in caves is constant year-round. It is generally the average annual mean temperature of the outdoor air. In other words, if the lowest typical temperature in the winter is 20 degrees Fahrenheit in the winter and the highest typical temperature is 90 degrees Fahrenheit in the summer, the cave temperature will tend to be 55 degrees - right in the middle.

So if the low temperature in an African village is only 40 degrees and the high is typically 90 degrees, we can expect the cave temperature to be 65 degrees year round.

In MODERATE temperature installations, we propose using a complex underground heat exchange system to transfer this year-round 65 degree temperature into the greenhouses.

We propose digging a long 'air processing pit' approximately 10 to 15 feet deep, before construction of the greenhouses above takes place. This pit will ideally be dug by a small steam shovel / ditch digging machine, if available. Once the pit is complete, the air duct system will be assembled in the pit. By making this pit very long, i.e. 200 feet or more, we can place multiple greenhouses alongside the pit.

This air duct system will feature interconnecting sections of plasticized metal duct work. These sections will aligned back and forth in a zigzag fashion, from one end of the pit to the other. The air will circulate throughout this maze giving it maximum exposure to the natural temperature of the earth. The temperature will transfer to the air, raising or lowering it to the ambient temperature of the ground.
Metal is used in the core of these duct material to draw in the cool temperature; a plastic covering is added to prevent rusting and build up of excessive moisture.

This long chain of air ducts will be connected at both ends to plastic duct pipes that lead up into the building. Turbo fans, powered by solar panels located on the roof of the greenhouse, will be used to PULL conditioned air up out of the ground, and PUSH exhaust air out of the building. This cave effect air will help maintain a median interior temperature in the greenhouse, one that will be conducive to growing plants, as well as providing a comfortable environment for the people working in the greenhouse.

We believe that this simplified air transfer system will dramatically reduce the need to burn wood or fossil fuel for heat in the wintertime and will make the buildings more comfortable and manageable in the summer heat. Of course, there will be the need for some additional heating during the winter months, particularly in the northern regions. This is addressed in Chapter 16.

Duct Work Considerations

The details of the duct work and the heat exchange system will have to be developed by industry experts. We cannot use traditional aluminum duct work, because it would generate mold. Our concern is that plastic duct work would not transfer enough of the ambient temperature to make a difference. One consultant has proposed tapping into the water table and using a water-based cooling system. These questions will best be answered by the building materials team.

Our main concern in the underground ducts is that once they are buried deep into the earth, they should survive for many, many years without significant decay. We want all structures built by WHT to have the longest lifespan possible, so materials selection will be critical. There will always be maintenance required, and there will be elements that have a much shorter lifespan, but the core structure and its supporting components need to be built for longevity.

Swamp Coolers for Arid Installations

In the desert or in extremely dry and hot regions of the world, traditional Evaporative or 'swamp' coolers will be our chosen method of cooling the greenhouse air. These are devices that cool air through the simple evaporation of water. We can power these coolers through a system of solar panels and storage batteries, and we can obtain the water from the build-in water storage tanks that will be built into each greenhouse facility.

It will be critical to adjust the translucency level of the ceiling tiles; in areas of intense and constant sun, we will need to scale back the opacity of the roof panels to minimize the amount of light and heat that are allowed to pass into the building. This will reduce the overall heat and minimize the amount of cooling that is required.

Insulation to Prevent Temperature Spikes

The difference in interior temperature between the daytime and nighttime hours will be significant; as soon as the sunlight fades, the temperature will plummet - and that will harm the plants. One solution is to use an interior 'cushion' of poly film. The following idea comes from the Greenhouse Experts website, (www.greenhouseexperts.com): "If you want to maintain an above freezing temperature in the structure all winter, then I would seriously consider an inflated double layer of poly film. This helps you save on long term heating costs because the layer of air between the sheets acts as an insulator and most of your heat loss occurs through your roof."

We are proposing to use a trapped air chamber between the two layers of frosted clear panels on the sides of the greenhouse to achieve this very effect. The air ducts leading from beneath the ground will feed into these chambers, and vents at the top of the chamber will open into the greenhouse facility. The moving air will act as a buffer against extreme and rapid changes in temperature. We may also need to look at creating a double-layer roof panel for the very reasons stated above - to minimize heat loss in the winter and vent out extreme heat spikes in the summer.

Additional Heat for the Winter Months

How do we provide additional heat in the winter months? In most areas of our greenhouse installations, there will be no electricity or natural gas available to burn heat. In many of these areas, firewood is a rare commodity. Also, solar panels will not generate enough wattage to power heating coils, so they will be of minimal use - plus, the coldest time of day will generally be at night when no solar power is generated.

We propose the addition of a central fire-fueled air heating unit at the end of the 'foyer' between the pod-quads (4 greenhouses joined by a central buffer room or hallway, discussed in Chapter 17.) The air returns from the underground air heating/cooling pipes for all four pods will feed into a cast-iron air heating chamber. Below this chamber will be a conventional fire box, a place to burn wood or other fuel. When the outside temperature is extremely cold, fuel will be burned in the firebox, and the air that is returning to the greenhouses from the underground pipes will be heated by the fire. A manual air bypass pipe and mixing switch should be incorporated in the design so the temperature of the return air can be controlled to some degree.

This cast-iron heating unit will be subject to rust, and since it will be underground it will likely be in contact with humidity throughout the year. We envision the need to replace these units every 20 to 25 years, so they will be considered a long-term consumable item. As discussed in Chapter 9, we hope to use recycled metals to reduce the cost of creating and replacing these major structural elements.

Fuel for the Fire Box

In many desolate areas of the world, especially Africa, the living conditions are so grim that almost all brush and tree growth has been eliminated. There simply is no firewood or fuel to burn for heat. In these areas, we propose an alternative method of creating fuel to burn in the fire boxes, specifically for greenhouse heating in the winter months. See Chapter 16, "Fuel for Cooking and Heating" for details.

The fire box will externally heat the air that is circulated through the sealed air system using low-wattage fans; this will prevent smoke from entering into the buildings.

Mechanical, Electrical and Plumbing Considerations

We propose that all mechanical, electrical & plumbing (MEP) elements be simplified to a very extreme level.

Mechanical

- **Fans.** Electrical fans will be required to move air. We propose the creation of a single turbo air transfer unit, built with extremely long-lasting bearings and motor. This 'plug and play' unit will be used in every single air transfer situation, in every building type developed by WHT. When the unit eventually wears out, we want replacement to be a simple and quick task that can be handled by local residents. The unit will be powered by 12V power, supplied by solar panels installed into the roof of the facility.

- **Solar Panels.** These will be modular units that will be sealed into an airtight clear plastic frame. The unit will feature a modular plastic connector plug that will be watertight as well. When the structure is built, a modular connecting cable will be run through the wall of the building up to the roof where the solar panels are to be installed. When a solar panel eventually ceases to operate, local residents can replace it easily.

- **Water Heating Panels.** (These panels will be installed on shower facilities, laundry facilities, kitchens, etc. - wherever hot water is needed; it is not needed in greenhouses.) We propose the creation of a watertight plastic panel that features standard in & out hose connections on either end. Inside the panel is a lattice of aluminum tubes that criss-cross the panel like a radiator. When installed on the roof of a structure, the sunlight will heat the interior of the panel, heating the aluminum tubes, which will heat the water. When a panel eventually wears out or becomes faulty, local residents can replace it easily.

To recap, we propose the development of all-new modular MEP components. By standardizing these components and streamlining their construction here in the states, we can minimize their net cost. There cannot be any pre-planned obsolescence to these parts, because there are no maintenance technicians out in the remotest parts of the world.

WHT can airlift boxes of replacement components every few years, but it is not practical to maintain a service force out in the field. We propose that an emergency supply of replacement parts be left with every community and village served by WHT. When a fan goes out in the middle of the summer heat, the plants inside the structure will not weather the high temperatures; if a local resident can replace the fan in less than an hour, the facility can remain in service at all times.

Summary - MEP Considerations

When an engineer reads this and says "it can't be done", WHT would prefer to respond, "it hasn't been done yet - *but it will be!*" There are expensive ways to accomplish anything, and we simply have to come up with ways to accomplish the same tasks inexpensively.

For example, let's say that a particular crop requires excellent drainage to grow properly. An engineer might propose an elaborate system of electrical pumps and drainage canals. WHT would respond, 'why not build the greenhouse floor with a slight incline, so the water drains out to one side of the building using gravitational force? The same goal is accomplished, but our solution is permanent and inexpensive. That is the kind of thinking we want all participants in WHT to apply.

Chapter 16 - Fuel for Cooking and Heating
(Discussion on a slightly unpleasant topic, but one that is necessary...)

There are no immediate sources of conventional fuel in the remotest parts of the world. In developed nations we have a grid of natural gas pipelines that we can easily tap into for fuel, but such easy access to fuel is not found in much of the world. The developed nations are attempting to develop alternative energy sources as a way to protect the environment and potentially reduce global warming.

The most popular alternative energy source - solar power - is still one of the most expensive methods of producing energy. Wind power comes in a close second, power generated by water current comes in third, and geothermal power is fourth. Far, far down the list of alternative energy sources, in terms of cost per BTU of heat generated, is methane gas. Methane gas? Doesn't that come from... yes, it does: dung, both animal and human. It's an unpleasant topic, and one that the 'green' power people have a huge PR problem with. Communities simply do not want collection facilities in their neighborhoods.

Mother Earth News, (www.motherearthnews.com) a so-called "hippie" publication that was started in the early days of nature conservation - back when the "back-to-nature" movement wasn't discussed in Fortune 500 publications - researched this subject quite fully in their January/February 1974 edition. In hindsight, the editors of this publication were easily 30 - 40 - even 50 years ahead of their time. In this article, they promoted a method of collecting chicken poop, placing it into a giant pressure-tight container, and mixing it into a 'slurry' that would generate methane gas. A pressure valve on the top released gas into storage tanks for future use. It was basically a 'free' source of bottled gas, similar to the liquid propane tanks we rent at the local convenience store or do-it-yourself home center.

Just how much methane gas could this system produce? The author states that, "our cow-manure-and-water slurry began producing gas a week after we half-filled our digester with waste. As a matter of fact, my father spent most of the fall scrounging up all the old propane, bottled gas and other pressure tanks he could find. On its initial loading, you see, our generator produced a steady 41 cubic feet of high-quality methane a day for almost three months. Since he didn't really have any use for the fuel (other than demonstrating to the curious that it would burn) and since he was loath to let it go to waste, dad figured he ought to store the gas in some way.

So he did... by pumping the methane into pressure tanks with his air compressor. A standard (approximately four feet long) propane bottle would hold four days' production of gas when the methane was compressed to about 200 pounds per square inch. Which meant, of course, that dad needed another tank every four days. Pretty soon, it seemed, he had the containers sitting all over the farm... Actually, our generator produced more (sometimes much more) gas than that on a really warm day."

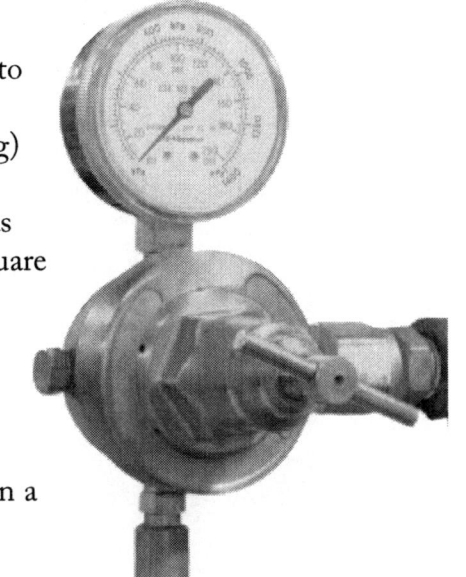

An added benefit is that the nitrogen-rich fertilizer left over from this process is just as valuable as the methane gas it makes, (see Chapter 27.)

We believe that the production and storage of methane gas in remote WHT facilities is the best fuel option, because it solves three rather challenging problems:

• **Waste Removal**. Communities produce waste, both human and animal. This waste is rarely put to good use. A collection system will benefit the living conditions as well as provide a source of fuel.

• **Burnable Fuel**. In many remote locations, firewood is a thing of the past. The trees have long been chopped down for lumber and fuel, and the new-growth trees rarely make it past bush size. Oil may be present deep in the earth, but no investment or technology is present to bring it to the surface - or if it is, the oil is siphoned off to tank farms and not made available to the poor people of the area. Communities WILL need burnable fuel for cooking, for heating of the facilities in the harsh months of winter, and for heating water all year round.

• **Fertilizer Production**. Once the waste products have been stripped of their methane-producing capacity, the by-product will also have been stripped of much of its unpleasantness. The residue, when mixed with compost, will make an excellent fertilizer for use in the growing facilities. It will be far more pleasant to work with than fertilizer made earlier in the degeneration process.

We propose the development of a unique collection system, as such:

1. **Toilet Facilities / Waste Storage Tanks**. Construct two or three in-ground collection tanks in a row. A set of tracks will run along either side of them. The toilet facility or 'outhouse', if you will, rolls along the tracks and is locked in place on top of the active tank. The tanks that are not in use will be sealed with a locking lid, similar to a pressure cooker. They will be generating methane gas when they are not in active use. The gas will be collected from this tank until the contents are no longer actively producing gas. At this point, the tank is opened, the contents are extracted for use as fertilizer, and the tank is ready for use again.

2. **Toilet Functionality**. Individual flaps will reside under the toilets. When the toilets are flushed, rainwater from the rooftop collection system will wash the effluent into the tank, and the flap will rise back up to form a tight seal. In this way, the odors will remain largely sealed inside the tank and the facility will be kept relatively odor free and more pleasant to use.

3. **Gas Collection**. When a tank becomes relatively full, the outhouse facility will be unlocked from that tank and rolled along the rails to a clean tank. The lid from the clean tank will be locked onto the full tank, and the process begins again.

4. **Bulk Access Door**. The outhouse structure will also feature a bulk access door. Effluent from the animal barns, chicken coops, etc., will be added through this door. Animal waste produces massive amounts of methane fuel.

Could it be that nature intended us to harness this natural source of heating and cooking fuel, and we have simply overlooked the opportunity? Desperate times call for desperate actions, and we need to fully explore ALL of our options for improving life on this planet. Let's keep our minds open to every one of the possibilities that surround us...

Chapter 17 - The 4-Greenhouse "POD"

To maximize the efficiency of the greenhouse design, we propose using a 4-greenhouse pod layout for all installations. Picture in your mind the number 5 as it is shown on a pair of dice: there are four dots on the perimeter and one dot in the center. In this proposal, the center dot represents an "air buffer" or entrance room. From this room, you gain access to any of the 4 greenhouses.

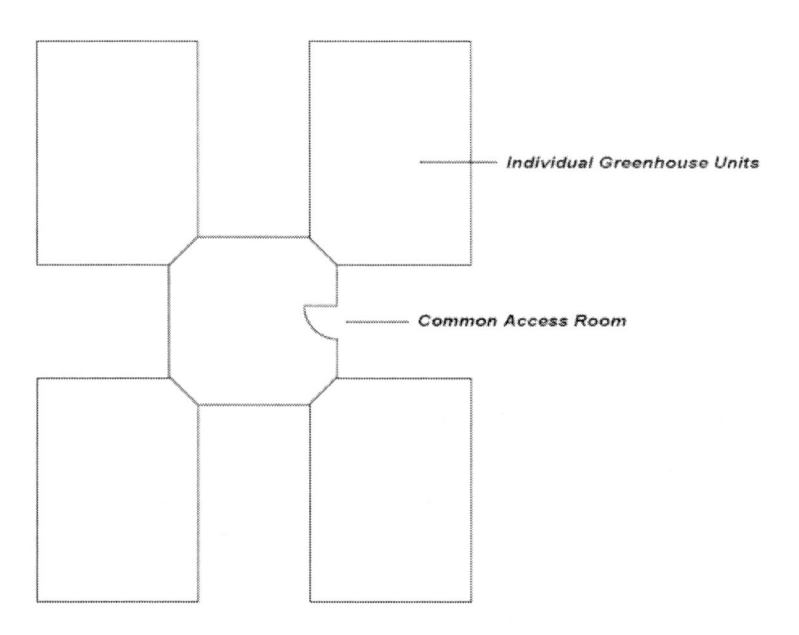

Individual Greenhouse Units

Common Access Room

The benefits of this design are many:

1. TEMPERATURE: If the outside environment is extremely hot or cold (as it will be much of the year in some locations), this buffer room prevents the outside air from reaching the plants. Plants hate sudden shifts in temperature. When the visitor enters this buffer room, he or she closes the outside door BEFORE opening any of the greenhouse doors. In times of extreme temperature, it may be wise to invoke a one-minute waiting period before opening the greenhouse doors. This will allow the air in the center chamber to re-acclimate, so when the greenhouse doors are opened it will not be as great a shock to the plants. For moderate-temperature installations, the underground 'cave effect' ductwork pit will run below the center of the four pods. Multiple pods can be constructed along one long pit, accelerating the speed at which these facilities can be constructed.

2. SECURITY: The only entrance to the pod will be through the center chamber; the outer walls of the greenhouse will have no entrance, so it will be extremely difficult for unauthorized personnel to gain access. This will also reduce the chance of wildlife gaining access to the greenhouses. The inner doors of the greenhouse can also be locked, so any potential thief will have to break two sets of locks to gain access to the food inside the buildings.

3. TOOL & IMPLEMENT STORAGE. The central chamber can be used to store gardening tools, fertilizer, boots, gloves, etc. This way, workers will have easy access to these items, regardless of which of the 4 greenhouses they are working in. A sink can also be installed in this central chamber for cleaning of tools, washing hands, etc.

I firmly believe that simple solutions are the best. The 4-greenhouse pod can be designed for quick, easy and consistent construction. Each pod can produce a large amount of food, and the planting schedule can be staggered so the pod will reliably feed "x" amount of people year-round. The number "x" will be the benchmark that we constantly seek to increase with testing and refinement of virtually all aspects of the program - construction design, materials, seed selection, soil selection and enhancement, fertilizer composition, watering amount, etc. The goal of the project is to incrementally increase "x" to the highest possible number over time.

The 4-pod system can become the workhorse solution of WHT in the battle against hunger. With the entire team working toward improving the success of the 4-pod system, remarkable gains can be achieved over time. A business case that pertains here is Southwest Airlines®; by using only one plane model across its entire fleet - the Boeing® 737 - the airline has maximized their efficiency and quality control. Simple solutions can truly be the best for long-term success.

Chapter 18 - Buildings: Unlimited Possibilities; Unlimited Challenges

Installation Options in Remote Locations

It's important to realize that some of the locations that need to be served will be very remote, such as high up in the Chilean mountains. There will be no way to get conventional freight trucks or heavy equipment to these types of locations. Therefore, we have two construction options:

1. Heavy Machinery. In easily accessed (non-remote) areas, WHT will use heavy equipment to dig the trenches for the air transfer system; this will be the quickest and easiest way to accomplish the goal. We will also have a drilling unit to dig water wells - whether the water table is 50 feet down or 500 feet down. Well water should always be accessed in our WHT communities whenever drilling is feasible.

2. Manpower Only. In remote or hilly areas, WHT will have to use hand tools or small gasoline-powered equipment. Digging the air transfer trenches will be a time consuming chore using a gas-powered tiller, but it will be better than attempting the job using shovels alone. Manpower will still be required to remove the dirt. In the initial digging, shovels can remove the dirt; as the hole gets deeper, a pulley system with a rope and bucket will be needed. The air transfer system will be a vital component of temperature control in the completed greenhouse, so this step cannot be bypassed. It will be almost impossible to dig a water well using gas-powered equipment, so this will likely not be possible in remote installations.

Building Codes: A Challenge Here in the States

The building codes in America were designed to protect the people living and working in the structures that make up our communities. That's a good thing, because strict adherence to these codes have saved countless lives. But these codes are based on commercially-viable ways of doing things, i.e. commercial HVAC units in every structure; sprinklers in commercial buildings, firewalls, plaster and concrete bricks with strict burn resistance and certification. The materials we will be using in our construction will likely not meet these codes, and thus will likely not be allowed in commercial building structures here in the U.S.

While this is a very good thing for the long-term safety of our citizens, it will not help us achieve rapid development of test facilities and food production domestically. We hope that a compromise can be achieved; one that meets the minimal requirements for human safety, yet allows us to maintain economy and simplicity in designing, building and testing these new facilities. Again, this one will be best solved by people with a deep understanding of the codes and ways to meet them. We do not anticipate code issues being a huge problem in the areas of greatest need such as Africa, Haiti, Mexico, South America, etc.

Greenhouses - Just the Start

In your wildest imagination, what types of buildings do you think WHT will need? We believe that the need will vary by community. It will vary by the types of crops that are preferred in each part of the world. It will also vary by the environmental conditions in each community. Here are some examples:

- **BASIC GREENHOUSE.** Ideal for growing tomatoes, green beans, cucumbers, squash and other fast-growing plants.

- **DEEP SOIL STRUCTURES.** Perfect for growing potatoes, peanuts, carrots, beets and other deep-root plants.

- **HIGH-MOISTURE STRUCTURES.** Imagine a huge indoor rice bed, with circulating water. Why not?

- **HIGH-CEILING / HIGH CAPACITY STRUCTURES.** Corn and wheat could be grown in a large structure, in controlled conditions.

Chances are, you balked when you saw "indoor rice bed". People have maintained OUTDOOR rice beds for countless generations. Why not replicate the success they've had for centuries? Well, bear in mind that water conditions are not the same in all parts of the world. Many locations are water-challenged. In a perfect world, communities could have an entire field of protected structures in which rice would be grown - WITHOUT CHANCE OF FAILURE! Imagine that: a GUARANTEED yield year after year, regardless of the weather, regardless of the rainfall, regardless of the storms and weather-related damage, and regardless of the pests and predators that interfere with the yield. But the cost! Won't it be ridiculously expensive to do this?

Removing the Massive Cost "Caveat"

Anything is possible, given enough money. But remember: we're talking about building all of this with trash. The soft drink bottles you generate in a month will make a brick. The bottle caps you generate in a year will make a foot of rebar. And the water bottles you generate in a year will make 10 square feet of roofing material. The core materials are all FREE. And once these structures are in place, they're not going anywhere: they will be in constant use for many, many years.

The cost of recycling the plastic, the transportation of the raw materials to the implementation country, the cost of the construction staff and supplies - it will all be amortized over the first year or two of the building's active use (and it will all be donated money, anyway.) From that point on, what you basically have is a 'FREE' building that nobody holds a mortgage on, and nobody can repossess. Sure, there will be some overhead in terms of maintenance and supplies - but it will be minimal.

What we are proposing is a long-term, cost-efficient solution to a major world problem. And it's the essence of why this is a viable, effective and timely solution to easing the world hunger crisis.

It would be easy to downplay the simplicity of these buildings, and say they are too primitive a solution. Yes, ideally, we would build traditional wood & brick structures around the world (after all, 1950's technology is tested and proven, isn't it?) And as such, each building would have a thousand different parts and elements, just as our conventional houses and commercial buildings do. And each one would cost at least $100,000 to build, it would require a team of 20 or 30 skilled workers and their accompanying costs and needs, and each one would take 6 months or longer to produce. Just ask yourself these five simple questions:

1. Who's going to pay for it?

2. Where are the materials going to come from? There are no trees in many undeveloped areas, so no wood to harvest! You'd have to ship these materials in from half way around the world!

3. Who's going to maintain them? We can't maintain or pay full-time staff members around the world, let alone ship in skilled workers.

4. Where is the electricity and water going to come from? There are no utilities to tap into in the remote regions of the world.

5. What on earth are you thinking???

Bear in mind that many of the people in these impoverished areas are living in shacks now. Their roofs leak, they have no heating or cooling. Their makeshift buildings often have no windows or doors. Many people are living under cardboard boxes - literally. So needless to say, the local residents are very open to suggestions and new ideas that could improve their living conditions. They will be very open to having workers come in and build facilities of any kind. The proposed WHT solution will allow us to build them waterproof, temperature controlled buildings in a few short weeks - buildings that will hopefully remain in service for decades to come. And we will do it without burdening them with a mortgage or a bill of servitude to pay for the structures in any way; we will build the structures and hand over the keys to the local leaders. It will almost be as if these buildings appeared out of nowhere - like manna in the desert!

It Costs No More To "Add a Little Style"

Architects are capable of creating remarkable designs. By adding a little flair here and there, a simple utility building can look very modern and appealing in design. We can incorporate a high degree of style and appeal in the buildings we create, and even use color to differentiate the buildings and add a sense of style.

To add color enhancements to the buildings, we can isolate the recyclable materials by color, i.e. keep green #2 plastic separate from yellow, white, clear, etc. Then, the separated material can be used to create colorized bricks. This would open up a wide range of design options during the construction process, so the buildings will have variety.

Imagine the benefits of multi-colored buildings:

-   Chickens who are now living under a tree will WELCOME the chance to come home to a bright orange henhouse.

-   Cows who are weathering the storms without a roof over their head will LOVE to come home to a glowing purple barn. (Purple cows... get it?)

-   Humans who now live in a thatch hut will be much more comfortable in a little pink house that they can call their own, (apologies to John Mellencamp; I just had to say it...)

And by the way, adding color to the plastics will also diminish the effects of UV rays and help prevent breakdown of the plastic. Through testing, we may learn to vary the amount of UV blockers we add to the plastic by individual country, to provide the exact level of protection the plants need against the harmful elements of the sun in their region.

The truth is, coloration can be added to any of the plastic materials we reclaim. We may discover through testing that tomatoes LOVE yellow-filtered light. Or, we may determine that the addition of a slight tint of cobalt blue to the greenhouse roof panels makes watermelons grow 10% larger. As we test more combinations, we will learn the winning approach to growing each individual crop - and that approach will be implemented around the world to maximize food yield in every WHT community. The possibilities - and the opportunities - are endless!

Advanced Greenhouse Construction Considerations - MICRO Farming

There are many successful techniques used by home and commercial gardeners that need to be explored by WHT researchers. These include:

- **Plant bed design & structure.** Using moveable bins vs. fixed. A moveable system would allow many more growing trays to be used vs. a fixed system. The trays would rotate via a slow motorized chain, similar to a Ferris wheel. It would allow each tray to receive direct light throughout the day.

- **Plastic lace for climbing plants.** Many climbing plants such as green beans, tomatoes and squash, will grow to huge heights if provided with a climbing surface. One idea is to use a plastic lace system, similar to the plastic holder on a six-pack of beverages. The lace will be produced in huge sheets and hung from the ceiling of the greenhouse down to the growing bed. The plant vines will grow up the lace and provide a tremendous growing area for the plants.

Fireproofing the Plastic Structures

One of the immediate concerns of the fire inspectors in approving the WHT building designs will be the flammability issue. Plastic is almost entirely made up of oil, and oil is of course very flammable. Plastic engineers will have to devise a formula to add flame resistance to the various plastic building materials. The bricks themselves will be filled with sand or dirt, so there is a degree of flame resistance present. But the plastic itself will have to be made flame retardant as well to prevent quickly-spreading fire and asphyxiation in the event of combustion.

VOC Issues Relating to Air Quality

Whenever plastic is used as a building material, an immediate concern is the issuance of organic gases or Volatile Organic Compounds (VOCs.) A definition of the problem is found on the United Stated Environmental Protection Agency (EPA) website, www.epa.gov/iaq/voc.html

"Volatile organic compounds (VOCs) are emitted as gases from certain solids or liquids. VOCs include a variety of chemicals, some of which may have short - and long-term adverse health effects. Concentrations of many VOCs are consistently higher indoors (up to ten times higher) than outdoors. VOCs are emitted by a wide array of products numbering in the thousands. Examples include: paints and lacquers, paint strippers, cleaning supplies, pesticides, building materials and furnishings, office equipment such as copiers and printers, correction fluids and carbonless copy paper, graphics and craft materials including glues and adhesives, permanent markers, and photographic solutions.

EPA's Total Exposure Assessment Methodology (TEAM) studies found levels of about a dozen common organic pollutants to be 2 to 5 times higher inside homes than outside, regardless of whether the homes were located in rural or highly industrial areas. Additional TEAM studies indicate that while people are using products containing organic chemicals, they can expose themselves and others to very high pollutant levels, and elevated concentrations can persist in the air long after the activity is completed.

Certain health effects are attributed to the presence of VOCs in living or working environment, including, per the EPA web site, "eye, nose, and throat irritation; headaches, loss of coordination, nausea; damage to liver, kidney, and central nervous system. Some organics can cause cancer in animals; some are suspected or known to cause cancer in humans. Key signs or symptoms associated with exposure to VOCs include conjunctival irritation, nose and throat discomfort, headache, allergic skin reaction, dyspnea, declines in serum cholinesterase levels, nausea, emesis, epistaxis, fatigue, dizziness."

The effects vary greatly based on the composition and quantity of VOCs in the air. Again, from the EPA web site: "The ability of organic chemicals to cause health effects varies greatly from those that are highly toxic, to those with no known health effect. As with other pollutants, the extent and nature of the health effect will depend on many factors including level of exposure and length of time exposed. Eye and respiratory tract irritation, headaches, dizziness, visual disorders, and memory impairment are among the immediate symptoms that some people have experienced soon after exposure to some organics. At present, not much is known about what health effects occur from the levels of organics usually found in homes. Many organic compounds are known to cause cancer in animals; some are suspected of causing, or are known to cause, cancer in humans."

There are simple ways to detect the levels of VOCs in the air, primarily the small hand-held devices known as Photoionization (PID) / Volatile Organic Compound (VOC) Detectors. It is our goal at WHT to monitor the level of VOCs present in the air within the structures we build, and to test possible ways to reduce these components in the breathable air in our buildings. Possible ways to reduce these pollutants are filtration, improved air circulation, sealants or coatings on the inner walls of the structure to prevent emissions from seeping inward, etc. In summary, WHT is aware of the potential problems in this area, and we are determined to identify and properly deal with the levels of VOCs in the construction of the buildings we make using recycled plastics.

Health Concerns Regarding BPA in Plastics

One concern that has been raised is the presence of the chemical **bisphenol A (BPA)** in the plastic products we use each and every day. BPA is used to harden plastics, but there are questions as to whether this chemical can leach out of food-storage containers and into the contents of the food. Studies of BPA have linked it to increased risks of diabetes, heart disease and infertility. The Food & Drug Administration (FDA) have taken the position that BPA is non-harmful. Some experts are cautioning consumers to look for food containers that have the recycling code of 7; such containers rarely contain BPA.

Our position at WHT is that while BPA issues should be researched in greater detail, they will not deter our efforts. We are using recycled plastics to build growing facilities, buildings and other implements, but the food we produce will all be fresh. The plants that we grow will not come into direct contact with the recycled plastic, so the issue of BPA transference will be unlikely to affect the fresh food that our facilities will produce.

Chapter 19 - MACRO Farming - The Key To Large-Scale Hunger Relief

While greenhouses and hothouses are good short-term / small-scale solutions to world hunger, a larger and more productive solution is needed as well. That is why we propose the use of Large-Grid Irrigation Plats, i.e. macro-farming. This is a large-scale farming solution that can potentially create a significantly larger yield than the micro-farming solutions we have previously discussed. In our proposed macro-farming solution, eight large plats are supported by a central water containment and distribution tank. We call it the 8-to-1 solution.

The 8-to-1 Solution.

We propose the creation of a 9-grid mini-pasture plat. Here is how it works:

- **THE GRID.** Shown below is a 9-box grid, similar to a tic-tac-toe board. Each box in the grid is approximately 100' x 100'. The center grid is actually a large water collection tank; the surrounding 8 grids are the actual growing plats. These plats are tilled, seeded and nurtured using standard farming methods. The only difference is that the plats are fed by a gravity-driven underground irrigation system, supported by the water collection tank.

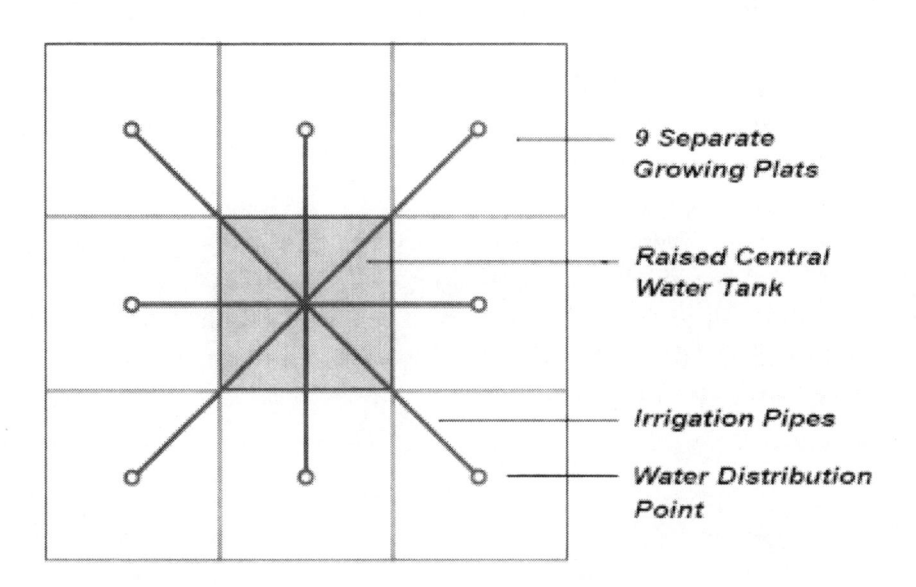

9 Separate Growing Plats

Raised Central Water Tank

Irrigation Pipes

Water Distribution Point

- **THE WATER SOURCE.** The center grid contains a huge water collection facility. The center grid is built on a raised dirt bed, approximately 8 to 10 feet higher than the surrounding grids. On top of this dirt bed, we build a base structure out a double-layer of our recycled plastic bricks. We use rebar to hold the structure in place, as well as cross-bars and retaining caps to contain the massive weight of the stored water. This structure becomes a giant water collection tank, capable of holding thousands of gallons of water.

- **WATER COLLECTION WINGS.** Spanning out from this tank is a series of plastic sheets, each section being 1 foot higher than the next. These sheets are supported by the posts made of the plastic bricks, giving them support when they are laden with rain water. The water trickles down the sheets into the collection tank. Because these 'wings' are made of clear plastic, light passes through them to the crops - so they do not block the sunlight needed by the plants.

- **WATER DISTRIBUTION.** The stored water is driven by gravity down to the 8 growing plats through a series of buried irrigation pipes. Cut-off valves allow the farmer to release the water as needed. *(In future incarnations, the water release can be computer-controlled using data collected from sensors placed in the growing fields.)* The water feeds into the buried irrigation pipes, which have drainage holes drilled throughout them. This allows the water to soak into the ground around the plants.

- **WATER RETENTION.** The tank will fill during the rainy season, and hold the water for use during the dry season. Cover panels can be added to minimize evaporation.

The net result: the plants receive water from a reliable source, 365 days a year, regardless of the weather conditions. The 8-to-1 solution assures that the crops will have water year in and year out, minimizing the potential for crop failure. And water, as we will discuss next, will be our #1 concern with every installation.

Chapter 20 - Water: The Key To Everything

Consider the problems facing farmers in the world's most destitute areas:
- Improper soil conditions
- Shortage of water
- Shortage of fertilizer
- Shortage of pesticides or other pest-repellants
- Lack of a consistent irrigation process

The largest of these needs is, of course, water. All of the best equipment, the best soil, an abundant supply of fertilizer, plenty of sun - all of these are diminished in value if there is no water available to keep the plants alive. You can have rain 48 weeks out of the year, but if you miss a full 4-week gap in the middle of the summer, your plants will burn up and die - yielding no food whatsoever.

That is why we propose to make rainwater collection a key tool in our fight against world hunger. There are three ways that we propose to collect rainwater:

1. **BUILT-IN WATER STORAGE TANKS** on the sides of all greenhouses / growing structures, all farm buildings including chicken coops and cattle barns, all community buildings including kitchen / commissary buildings, and even the housing structures. The roofs of these facilities will be angled, and will drain into conventional gutters, which will lead into storage tanks built into the sides of the structures. The tanks will automatically fill each and every time it rains. With these tanks, substantial amounts of water can be stored for year-round use - even if the area only receives significant rainfall a few days out of the year.

2. **LARGE COMMERCIAL FARMING WATER STORAGE TANKS** in the center of an 8-to-1 grid (see Chapter 19.)

3. **UNDERGROUND TANKS.** These will be fed by culverts and drainage ditches. This water is the 'emergency source' to be used in times of deepest drought.

Water Collection System

Water is becoming a scarce commodity in much of the world. Global warming is likely the cause, but without getting into that debate, suffice it to say that in many impoverished areas there is no steady supply of clean water. One feature that we propose building into every WHT structure is a rainwater collection system. Here's how it works:

- Gutters are added to the drainage sides of all roofs; roofs are angled down toward the gutters.

- The gutters are at a slight angle to one side of the building.

- An enclosed collection tank is built into the side of each structure. It is wide enough for a person to crawl into (for quarterly or bi-annual cleaning). As the building is being constructed, the interior of this tank will be sealed with spray-on melted plastic, creating a solid 1/8" thick lining to the tank. A spigot on the outside of the tank allows the water to be drawn out.

- The gutters flow into a collection / debris removal funnel just above the tank. The flowing water turns a device that removes leaves, twigs or other debris that could clog the intake spout. It also opens the entry valve to the tank, which remains closed if no water is flowing.

- The rainwater is collected into the tank; it can be used for watering the plants, washing clothes or bathing, or it can boiled or treated for human consumption and cooking.

- Additives will need to be poured into the tank on a regular basis to prevent algae build-up and maintain the potability of the water. It will be up to the chemistry team to determine the proper additive that will maintain the freshness of the water without inhibiting the viability of the water as nourishment for the plants. Also, scheduled draining and scrubbing of the tank will be required to keep the lining of the tank clean.

- The in-greenhouse tank could potentially hold upwards of 1,000 gallons of water, depending on the width. If these tanks are built into every building constructed in the village, the people could reasonably have 5,000 or 10,000 gallons of water available after the rainy season. This could potentially give them sufficient water for up to 6 months without rainfall.

It would be ideal to have a more sophisticated water collection and storage system in place in each of these villages. And if well water is available in abundant supply, there will be little need for collecting rainwater. But if water is in short supply at the site, a collection and storage system - designed and constructed properly - could provide a permanent, safe, and effective way of collecting and storing precious fresh water to meet the daily needs of the community. Plus, the water will be available immediately at the site, with no need to haul it for miles on end from a remote well or stream.

Drip Irrigation

Perhaps the best way to assure that the plants in every greenhouse will be watered every day is by installing automated drip irrigation systems in every facility. I believe that these systems can be controlled mechanically, avoiding the major problems that are likely to occur with electronically-controlled systems:

1. Electrical failure, due to component fault or lack of electrical current in the battery system.

2. Improper settings or manual error in setting of the timer,

3. Failure to open the water supply. To remedy this, we could create a slow-release drip valve that gradually fills a small storage tank from the main water storage tank on the side of the greenhouse. As the small tank fills, it raises a float (similar to that found in a commode.) When it reaches the top, a mechanical switch is triggered that releases the water slowly through a drip pipe into the plant beds. When the small water tank is empty, the release switch shuts and the process repeats itself.

Using this type of crude mechanical float and switch mechanism, we can be assured that the plants will be watered on a consistent basis - even if the greenhouse managers are detained elsewhere, or simply neglect their duties in caring for the plants.

Our goal here is not to diminish the role of the greenhouse manager - it is simply to assure that the plants thrive and continue to produce fruit - regardless of human error, social/political conditions, and regardless of the level of attentiveness provided by the local workers.

Alternative Water Sources / Growing in Arid Seaside Environments

Some very exciting developments are being generated by the Seawater Greenhouse company of London, England, (www.SeawaterGreenhouse.com).

According to the company's website, "The Seawater Greenhouse is a unique concept which combines natural processes, simple construction techniques and mathematical computer modeling to provide a low-cost solution to one of the world's greatest needs - fresh water. The Seawater Greenhouse is a new development that offers a sustainable solution to the problem of providing water for agriculture in arid, coastal regions.

The process uses seawater to cool and humidify the air that ventilates the greenhouse and sunlight to distill fresh water from seawater. This enables the year round cultivation of high value crops that would otherwise be difficult or impossible to grow in hot, arid regions."

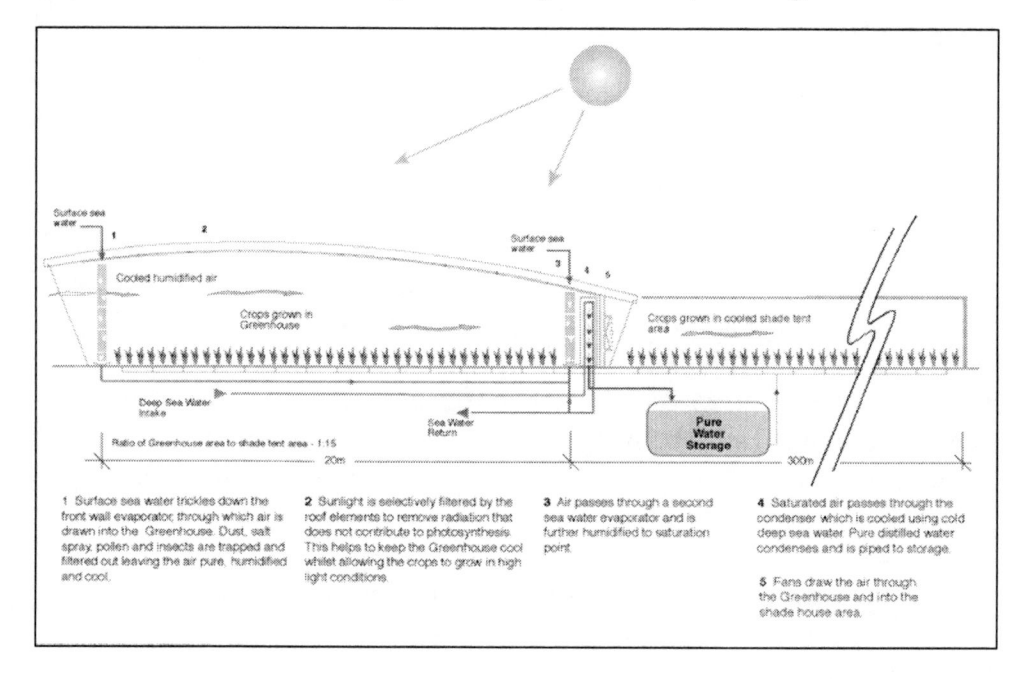

The company's approach is remarkable in that it provides a sustainable source of both food and fresh water where little to none exists today. Their facilities are built in seaside or island-based communities that have limited or no sources of potable water, but have ready access to unlimited quantities of salt water - which traditionally has been too costly to desalinate. "Although seawater is abundant, conventional desalination consumes substantial energy, usually derived from fossil fuels. There is a need for affordable and sustainable means of producing food and water, without reliance on energy reserves," according to its website.

In speaking with Charlie Paton, Managing Director of Seawater Greenhouse, he informed me that his greenhouses must be constructed of glass, because plastic would decompose too rapidly in the sun. In his testing, he found that plastic was not a reliable material for greenhouse exteriors, based on the damaging effects of ultraviolet (UV) light from the sun. And this leads us to our next topic...

Breakdown of Plastic Materials Due to Sunlight Exposure

According to Mr. Paton, "While it is true that buried plastic does not break down, if it is exposed to sunlight, it breaks down very quickly - from a few months to a few years. If we could use recycled plastic to build our greenhouses we would, but sadly it is not viable. It is primarily the UV in light that breaks down plastic," he said. When asked if there were treatments that could be added to the plastic to prevent this decomposition in the sunlight, he stated "There are additives that extend the life such as carbon or TiO_2, and of course the thicker the material, the longer it will last. But also, various additives leach away and cause the plastic to become brittle. Bury it away from sunlight and yes, it does not break down," he said.

Additionally, "The very best available, UV stabilized polythene we use in the Middle East to cover our greenhouses fails after 3 years. ETFE (a type of transparent teflon) lasts 15-20 years or more but is hugely expensive and is not recyclable. Even the black polyethylene irrigation pipe can turn to dust in 10 years. Timber on the other hand will last indefinitely if kept dry and free from termites, and glass is pretty good," he said.

Mr. Paton's advice has led us to investigate ways to mitigate this natural breakdown of the plastic materials caused by the harmful effects of ultraviolet (UV) light.

Additional research on this subject was presented in the February 12, 2009 edition of <u>Scientific American</u>, in an article titled, **"Putting the "Green" into Greenhouses"** by Jeanne Erdmann. It specifically addressed greenhouse heating and cooling options, and ways to make greenhouses more environmentally friendly by cutting down on their energy use. Some of the key points are:

• Using layers of ultraviolet treated plastic on the outside of the greenhouse to protect the plastic from being broken down by sunlight.

• Designing a specially curved roof on the greenhouse; the curve focuses light on clusters of solar cells... The curve acts like a magnifying glass, concentrating the sunlight on the cells so that it is 30 times stronger. Motors powered by the solar cells in turn move large actuator arms to reposition the solar cells to follow the sun in its track across the sky, thereby achieving the most efficient angle year-round.

• Using an outer wrap of two layers of plastic with a 'dead air zone' between them. Little blowers inside the greenhouse called puffer fans blow air through tubing nestled inside the two layers of plastic. The fans run 24 hours a day to maintain a dead air space that helps insulate the greenhouse by keeping temperatures around 65 degrees Fahrenheit (18 degrees Celsius) and protects plants from temperature fluctuations.

• In the summer, workers spray on white paint with a chalky consistency that is specially made to reflect sunlight but is easy to remove. As the colder winter months set in they scrub it off with push brooms.

These are all excellent ideas and should be considered for testing in the WHT design scenarios.

Deflecting UV Rays with Laminates

There have been significant developments in this area by plastics scientists. One such invention is a Polarized Plastic Laminate invented and patented by Michael Barry Smith of Thousand Oaks, CA. He has developed a 5-layer film that, according to the patent documentation, provides: (1) impact resistance; (2) scratch resistance; (3) craze resistance; (4) resistance to chemical or environmental deterioration; (5) flex accommodation; (6) easy dyeability in a variety of colors; (7) good optical properties; (8) the ability to be easily manufactured in a variety of shapes; and (9) low cost. We are investigating this product and other options to solve the deterioration problem in the exterior plastic components of our greenhouses.

The topic of using plastic materials in gardening and growing facilities has been bandied about for years, with mixed opinions. I found an interesting post on the online 'BonsaiTalk' forum. Here, the issue was whether or not to use recycled plastic as a base for growing bonsai trees.

One writer wrote, "Polystyrene, however, is a very unstable plastic to use for bonsai applications. It breaks down pretty quickly, especially out in the sun. UV rays disintegrate polystyrene quickly. First it fades, then it crumbles. This can take a couple of months to a year. Sooner or later, though, it will crack, crumble or turn to whitish dust."

Another writer from the Netherlands, "Weeijk", who works in the plastics industry writes, "That's why I will use UV stabilized coloured "masterbatch" (little pieces of plastic with high amount of pigment (40-50% and additives like UV stabs). Normally the "masterbatch" we make in our plant has sunlight exposure values which are guaranteed for 10 years. The "masterbatch" is then mixed with blanc Polypropylene in an amount of 2-3% and melted. With the melted substance of about 200 degrees C, I create the slab. This is probably too far down in the material for some, but after all, it's my job."

Current Environmental Applications for Recycled Plastic

Recycled HDPE plastic is currently being used to create huge floating balls, which are placed into lakes to prevent birds from congregating there for a variety of health & safety-related issues. Some residents around these lakes have been concerned about the possible leaching of pollutants from the HDPE.

One writer to a blog in California, "Mr. HDPE Pellet", writes: "There are clearly other issues here beyond HDPE that I am unqualified to comment. But I do know something about HDPE. The degradation of

HDPE that occurs in the presence of sunlight is a determination of the physical strength of the polymer and color of the polymer; additives are used to maintain these properties. However, even if completely unstabilized the new balls and aged balls would not leach anything into the water. It is a simple issue of:

1) hydrophobic polyethylene, and:
2) the molecular weights of the polymer involved (several hundred thousand).

That leaves the additives… the balls are black, indicating the use of carbon black as a stabilizer (like in tires). The carbon black is a very, very effective thermal and light stabilizer (free radical trap) that is not going to leach from the polymer as it is also hydrophobic."

In fact, the use of additives or composite materials in the manufacturing process can provide a multitude of benefits, as evidenced by many products in commercial production today.

Additives and Composite Materials that Increase Product Strength and Durability

It's no secret that the use of recycled plastic in building materials is a growing industry trend. Look around in any community and you will see plastic park benches, parking stops, dock bumpers, fences, decks and more. The benefits are significant: beams and blocks of recycled plastic are waterproof, mold-resistant, maintenance-free, defect-free, extremely long-lasting and easy to work with. In fact, the construction industry loves this material.

Here are just a few examples of the many advancements being made by manufacturers of recycled plastic building materials.

LifeTime Lumber (http://www.ltlumber.com)
This company makes timber from polyurethane. From its website: "Polyurethane chemistry is used in a wide variety of industrial and

consumer applications because it has the ability to provide a unique combination of weight, strength, hardness, flexibility and resistance to water absorption. The filler material used in the process is fly ash generated from the use of coal to produce electricity. Our ash is a non-hazardous mineral particle residual of the coal combustion process used as a mineral filler in many other building materials such as concrete, cement blocks, bricks, tiles and other products. Its unique physical and chemical properties lend it to many recycling applications."

PlasticLumberYard (http://www.plasticlumberyard.com)

This company produces a plastic roofing material that has a 50-year warranty. From its website: "Engineered using the most advanced technology in material development and manufactured from a proprietary fire rated ACE Compound, This is the only synthetic roofing slate of its kind. Its unique base - ACE Compound, is an extremely durable, impact resistant and heat resistant thermoplastic... **The Material:** Plastic Authentic Roof's uncontaminated ACE Compound base is meticulously blended with an unrivaled UV protection package and vital FR (flame retardant) additives ensuring that that they are both locked in securely and thoroughly combined together... **UV Protection:** Plastic Authentic Roof has been tried and tested to stand up to this challenging task. Its composite base offers a 15,000 hour direct Arizona sun exposure protection package. The unrivaled dual UV package embedded within our slates is among the best in the world. **Flame Resistance:** Plastic Authentic Roof is the ultimate shield to protect any home or building; this is fortified by its "CLASS A" flame rating for the slates alone. No special underlayment is required. UL tested and certified. **Impact Resistance:** Plastic Authentic Roof is virtually indestructible. Even the strength of the elements are no match. Plastic Authentic Roof offers the highest category impact testing available: Class 4 (UL 2218). This again solidifies its perfect fit with any home or building, particularly in extreme weather areas. Whether it's HAIL or even a HAMMER, it doesn't matter."

FiberForce® Plastic Lumber (http://www.plasticboards.com)
This company makes lumber using recycled high density polyethylene plastic, colorants, ultraviolet stabilizers, combined with fiberglass. According to its website, "this combination provides better structural properties (strength and rigidity) for more demanding applications. FiberForce has clear advantages over composite lumber products for structural plastic lumber applications. FiberForce is low maintenance and does not require painting or staining. (It) will not rot and is resistant to oils, chemical, saltwater, termites, marine borers, and fungi."

American Composite Timbers (http://www.compositetimbers.com)
In an innovative combination of materials, this company uses composite construction to create plastic building materials. From its web site: "In simplistic terms, a composite is defined as the combining of two distinct materials in such a way that neither material completely merges with the other and the combination creates a system that provides benefits like improved strength, dimensional stability, and superior durability. Fiber-reinforced polymer (FRP) composites are defined as the incorporation of a reinforcement (such as fiberglass) into a polymer (plastic) matrix such that the reinforcement offers a discernible reinforcing function in one or more directions. ACT Composite Plastic Lumber is manufactured using FRP composite technology that combines all of the inherent benefits of plastic for long-term durability with reinforcements that provide strength characteristics common to wood."

"Composite" building construction is not a new concept. For thousands of years, civilizations throughout the world have used basic elements of their surrounding environment in the fabrication of dwellings. For instance, "bricks" were made from mud and straw with the mud acting much like the resin in fiber-reinforced polymer (FRP) composite construction and the straw acting as reinforcement to hold the brick together during the drying (and shrinkage) process. What FRP composites can "bring to the table" is a versatile material system that can be formulated to be nearly impervious to all environmental factors while also being environmentally-friendly."

American Recycled Plastic, Inc. (http://www.itsrecycled.com)
This company mixes recycled HDPE (#2 milk jug material) with fiberglass to create a variety of wood-like products. From its website: "Structural plastic lumber shall be manufactured with HDPE and

fiberglass elements to act reinforcing with the HDPE. Lumber shall be molded in one piece per specified size. All materials will have UV additives to prevent deterioration of the plastic lumber from exposure to UV light. HDPE will be made up of no less than 80% of recycled materials; both post industrial and post consumer. Finished plastic lumber will not rot, split, crack or splinter for a minimum of 50 years. It shall be resistant to termites, marine borers, salt spray, oil, and fungus."

The company's motto is a fitting summary for the advantages of using recycled plastic in building materials: *"Your Plastic Debris Will Save a Tree!"*

The reason I've listed these companies is not to promote them or their products; it is to show that many companies today are producing viable commercial building products out of recycled plastic. If a company can make roofing material out of plastic and give it a 50-year warranty, it proves that it can be done. It's not a question of viability; it's a question of cost, chemistry, and logistics. If a company can make plastic lumber that also carries a 50-year warranty, it proves that the manufacturing world can produce a quality product out of recycled plastic. It proves that there are genuine benefits as well as great value in using recycled plastic as a building material.

And where there are great benefits and value to be found, there are investments being made to improve the durability, strength and performance of these materials. It is our intention to solicit the participation of these manufacturers in the development of the materials we will use in constructing our greenhouses. There is no need to 'reinvent the wheel': industry has already solved many of the problems inherent in using recycled plastic as building materials. By participating with WHT in our mission to solve world hunger, these manufacturers stand to gain millions of dollars in advertising and public relations gains - bringing them additional exposure to consumer, business and government sales.

It will be a challenge to get companies such as these to participate in the WHT mission, especially in our early phase. We believe that this challenge will become easier once plastics industry leaders such as DuPont and Exxon/Mobil endorse our mission. And once we have the backing of major plastics industry organizations such as the SPE - Society of Plastics Engineers, and the SPI - Society of the Plastics Industry, news of our work will spread rapidly. It will make it far easier for us to arrange working partnerships with top manufacturers and obtain additional research financing.

Chapter 21 - Growing Food

Food Plan Implementation - 5 Phases

We anticipate 5 distinct phases in the food production process.

1. STARVATION PREVENTION. The goal here is to establish one or more greenhouses to produce the greatest amount of sustenance in the shortest amount of time. Plants will be selected that have the greatest food output per square food, with the shortest germination time. We anticipate that this will include bean sprouts, sweet peas, lettuce, etc.

2. SUSTAINABLE SUSTENANCE. The next phase will be to grow plants that produce high-yields on an ongoing, daily basis. These will likely include plants such as green beans, tomatoes, squash, and other quick-growing, high-yield crops.

3. NUTRITIONAL DIVERSITY. The next phase will be to add plants and vegetables that significantly enhance the nutritional value of the diet. The plants selected will typically have a longer germination time, longer growth time, or lower yield, but will add variety to the product mix. This may include such items as corn, rice, peanuts, eggplant, melons, onions and other high-output crops. As we advance into nutritional diversity by adding additional greenhouses to a community, the speed at which the plants grow becomes less and less critical. At that point, the nutritional value and popularity of the food product takes on increasing importance.

4. FOOD ENHANCEMENTS. As the community becomes established nutritionally, they will want further enhancements to their diet and a return to the foods that are native to the area. Note that if these items are quick growing, they will be added early in the development plan. The items might include garlic, peppers, spices and herbs, as well as plants and roots that are used in the making of condiments and sauces. A good example of this would be the tamarind, which is not an edible fruit, but is very important in making sauces that add flavor and depth when added to food as it cooks.

In many countries of the world, food that is not spiced properly is not desirable, so having these enhancements available when cooking is more than just a preference; it's a fundamental element of the regional culture and lifestyle.

5. COMMERCIAL FARMING. After the community's own food needs are met and the structures are producing more food than the community needs, commercial food production can be implemented. Here, the community sells its surplus goods on the common market to raise capital for expansion and improvement of the community.

Chapter 22 - The Basics: Soil

On the surface, this may seem like an odd topic to discuss. Soil is soil, isn't it? Actually, all soil in all parts of the world is unique. Some soils are nutrient-rich, full of the elements that plants need to grow and thrive. Other soils are nutrient-depleted, and provide little to none of the elements that plants need to survive.

Because WHT communities will be established throughout the world, we believe that soil analysis and rehabilitation will be a long-term effort - and one that will be different in every single installation. In essence, one entire category of developing a community will be creating and enhancing the local soil to make it usable as a growing base in the greenhouses. This may take a few short weeks in some areas, and many, many years in other areas; it will depend on several factors:

- **History of the soil.** Has it been worked / overworked?
- **Origins of the soil.** Is it riverbed soil, receiving nutrients from other locations, or has it been stagnant for many years?
- **Chemical analysis of the soil.** What elements are present? Which chemical properties are dominant, which are lacking?

Soil can be brought back to life through the addition of chemicals and soil enhancers such as peat, manure, and other common products. Soil can be conditioned by adding earthworms, which process the soil and make it more conducive to supporting plants. But all of these steps require time, patience and ongoing attention and monitoring. In many of the WHT communities, we simply will not have the luxury of that time; we will need to start growing mass quantities of food in the shortest-possible timeframe.

That is why we are proposing to use man-made or 'artificial' soil. There are a great many of these products being produced today, and they offer a distinct advantage in a controlled growing environment: they are predictable. In other words, we know what to expect from them on an ongoing basis, and what NOT to expect from there. By using an artificial soil, we can manipulate the nutrients, humidity and temperature to provide the ultimate growing substrate.

One interesting product that is indicative of the type of soil we propose using is called "Millennium Soil™." It is a registered, trademark product of an inventor based in Texas named Craig VanPelt. In an interview, Mr. VanPelt described his product as follows:

"Millennium Soil™ is a totally safe, non-toxic and environmentally friendly material that starts out in crystal form. When the Millennium Soil™ crystals come in contact with water, each crystal acts as a powerful sponge, absorbing hundreds of times it weight in water. As the crystals absorb water, they actually "grow" to about the size of a nickel, and appear like globules of crystal clear white Jell-O®," says VanPelt. The roots of plants or vegetables growing in Planter Pouches filled with Millennium Soil™ penetrate the globules of gel, and are able to absorb water and nutrients as required.... No watering too much.... or too little. And now plants can be shipped via ground service, without worry of them dying along the way.

Another advantage of using this soil is its long-term stability. According to Mr. VanPelt, "Studies show that Millennium Soil™ will keep working for more than 25 years. As the plant roots take water out of the Millennium Soil™ the gelatin-like chunks will reduce in size. Then, when additional water is added, the Millennium Soil™ "rehydrates" and the gelatin-like chunks grow once again."

Plants thrive in this type of artificial soil, because it presents the moisture and added nutrients in a way that plants actually prefer over natural soil. Again, per Mr. VanPelt, "plant roots burrow into the chunks of Millennium Soil™, and the roots then act like straws, and can take water as needed. Actually, the Plant "decides" when it needs water. This is especially important, since most plants die because we "over-water" or "under-water" them," he said. To find out more, please visit http://www.dirtfree-maintenancefree.com.

Artificial soil from recycled materials

There are many new alternatives to natural soil, each with unique features and benefits. Here is a patent for an artificial soil with elements that can be altered to meet the needs of different climates and crops:

United States Patent 5472475
Abstract: "To make an artificial topsoil combine by hand or in a blending machine, by volume, either dredged river silt, sand or basalt, and cellulose from recycled paper or yard waste, with composted animal or human waste for general reclamation and cereal crops, or vegetable or fruit residuals for gardens or potting soil, and then add calcium in the form of calcium silicate as slag or lime and ammonium nitrate or sulfate mixed with water, and then charcoal or equivalent amount of phosphorus, sodium, and sulfur as are present in charcoal. This combination of material replicates the calcium base, decaying cellulose, silt and animal or vegetable waste structure of natural soils.

Various soil types can be duplicated by adjusting the base content of sand, silt, or basalt and rearranging the nutrient and mineral content to compensate for differing levels of each, for example: calcium and organic percentages should be increased to maximum when using sand as a base. Calcium should be decreased to the minimum percentage when using silt or basalt as a base. Rhyolite should also be added when available to compliment basalt. These elements can be combined to match local soil profiles, and then add seeds are that are appropriate to yield the areas naturally occurring foliage or crop preference."

This is just one of hundreds and perhaps thousands of soil alternatives that have been developed and need to be reviewed for possible inclusion in the WHT program. Cost will play a large role, as we must test the return on investment vs. using natural soil, which is of course free.

Soil Depletion and Revitalization

You've heard the classic farmer's story that land needs to be "rested" from season to season. A farmer will grow wheat for 3 or 4 seasons, and then grow sugar cane to increase soil fertility. In a controlled greenhouse or hothouse environment, the soil will become depleted rapidly unless it is rotated with new soil or supplemented with chemical additives. By using artificial soil, this need to replenish the nutrients can be reduced or eliminated - simply because the soil's components provide the nutrient's directly. The soil will become depleted just as natural soil would, but the chemical and nutrient balances can be monitored and the soil's viable life can be easily determined.

Another approach, and one that is far more natural and economically appealing is the use of **Soil Carbonization**. The Discovery Channel has presented a very compelling documentary about soil in the Amazon rain forest. As early as the 1870's, archaeologists visiting the Amazon were curious as to why patches of dense forest with rich, black soil would be surrounded by areas of pale yellow clay soil that was so infertile it would support little more than the native weeds. How could such a dichotomy exist?

The answer was found when researchers discovered clay pottery shards in the rich, black soil areas. Up to 10% of the soil was found to contain pottery shards, leading the black earth to become known locally as ("terra preta do indios" ("black earth of the Indians.") Upon analysis, the soil was found to contain significant levels of charcoal. Apparently the natives discovered the benefits of burning their farm waste, i.e. 'carbonizing' it, and then grinding it into a fine powder before returning it to the soil. The very richest soils were found to contain between 9 and 40 percent carbon.

In the past, scientists largely assumed that this carbon was inert and its contributions to the soil content were largely mechanical, i.e. adding bulk. But today, scientists have uncovered the relationship between this carbonization and the fertilization of plants.

An excellent resource that explains this phenomenon has been established by Scott Bidstrup, http://www.bidstrup.com/carbon.htm. His essay is titled, "Saving The Planet While Saving The Farm - *How soil carbonization could save the planet while it restores agricultural profitability.*" In this essay, Bidstrup explains the complex relationship between plants and carbon molecules:

"What the soil scientists, working with microbiologists, discovered was that a community of bacteria exists in symbiosis with the root hairs of plants in terra preta soils. The bacteria produce enzymes that release the mineral ions trapped by the heat-stabilized plant resins in the charcoal and make it available to the root hairs of the plant as nutrients. In return, the plants secrete nourishment for the bacteria. Not only that, but the resins within the charcoal act like an ion exchange resin, adsorbing traces of mineral ions onto the charcoal particle surfaces from the rain water, and trapping it within the charcoal's molecular structure, where it can be held for centuries - until the soil bacteria associated with a root hair come along and secrete the enzymes necessary for it to be released once again.

"So the trace minerals always present in rainwater actually act as a fertilizer - providing the nutrients needed by the crops, year after year. The secret of the soil fertility of the terra preta was finally understood. And it was understood how the indigenous farmers were able to produce bumper crops year after year, decade after decade without a single application of chemical fertilizer and without wearing out the soil."[4]

To harness the widespread gain that soil carbonization could bring to the farming industry, Bidstrup proposes that large-scale factories be built for the sole purpose of carbonizing plant by-products. Again, quoting his website, "The soil carbonizing business would own farms where kenaf, bamboo, switchgrass and other high-biomass crops are grown as a feedstock, or be located near sugar cane crushing mills, where large amounts of baguase (crushed cane fiber from which the juice has been extracted) is available cheap or for free as a feedstock for the charcoal production process."

This process can work hand-in-hand with alternative bio-fuel projects. To reduce America's dependence on fossil fuel and foreign suppliers, states have begun taking action to grow crops that can be converted into fuels, much as corn and sugarcane are converted into ethanol.

One of the crops that Bidstrup mentions as an excellent candidate for soil carbonization, switchgrass, is in essence a weed-like plant that is exceptionally hardy and requires almost no maintenance to grow. It is so hardy, in fact, that the State of Tennessee is centering a massive five-year $70 million program on it.

[4]*Copyright Scott Bidstrup. Used by permission.*

The Tennessee Biofuels Initiative is a five-year commitment of $70 million by the state over the next five years for bioenergy research and a demonstration program that includes construction of a pilot biofuels refinery that will be built in Vonore, Tenn. For more information visit http://www.utbioenergy.org/TNBiofuelsInitiative

A story in the Knoxville (TN) News Sentinel states that the initiative's goal is to plant 800 acres of switchgrass in the spring of 2008, with an additional 2,000 acres planted the following spring, and another 4,000 acres planted in 2010. The biofuels plant will have the capacity to produce 5 million gallons of cellulosic ethanol annually. When operating at full capacity, it will require about 170 tons of biomass per day. Those farmer incentives also include money to develop a seed industry for switchgrass in Tennessee.

There's not a lot of seed available to grow switchgrass, and that's because there hasn't been a lot of demand for it, according to Kelly Tiller, director of external relations for the biofuels initiative and an assistant professor of Agriculture Economics at the University of Tennessee. Planning and construction of several cellulosic ethanol plants are under way now across the country. The U.S. Department of Energy announced in February $385 million in funding for cellulosic ethanol production plants in Missouri, Florida, California, South Dakota, Virginia, and Colorado. The plants aim to use a range of feedstocks, including agricultural residues such as wheat straw, barley straw, corn stover and rice straw, as well as wood and switchgrass.

Two Birds / One Stone

It appears that the classic "two birds / one stone" story could come true with the use of these alternative crops:

a. FUEL can be extracted from the crops.

b. CHARCOAL can be harvested from the waste products of the fuel extracting process. This charcoal can be added to farm soil to create an extremely robust substrate for enhancing local soil in which to grow food.

The process is known as **pyrolysis**, in which biomass is burned at a high temperature in the absence of oxygen. The process yields both a charcoal by-product that can be used as a fertilizer, and bio-oil, which is a mix of oxygenated hydrocarbons that can be used to generate heat or electricity.

Do you see a connection here - how the scientific and agricultural communities are finally starting to see synergies and genuine viability and profitability in alternative approaches to both farming and fuel production? Ironically, by looking back in time to the ancient civilizations of the Amazon rain forest, we are learning ways to save our planet from the effects of our own 'modernization'. History can truly repeat itself, but we must be open to learning the lessons it is trying to teach us.

Further information about the development of "agrichar" as it has come to be known, can be found on the website of the Scientific American magazine (http://www.scientificamerican.com) keyword "agrichar" as well as the website of the International Biochar Initiative, http://www.biochar-international.org.

Chapter 23 - The Basics: Crops

There will always be a tradeoff between which crops the local people want to eat, vs. the crops that need to be grown. There is no question that everyone involved with a WHT greenhouse will have an opinion of what we SHOULD be growing vs. what we ARE growing. The real question becomes one of control, mission and necessity. *What do the people NEED to survive?*

In selecting which crops to grow in the various implementations of WHT growing facilities, we need to address the food health of the community. What is the food supply situation at this time? Here are three likely scenarios:

a. Food is plentiful, but the people have no money to purchase it. This is more of a political and/or agri-business question - not a greenhouse question. If WHT begins growing food and giving it to people for free, the local farmers and retailers will likely rebel against our efforts. This could require diplomatic intervention and the involvement of the local government. Some countries may rebel against our efforts and ban WHT from their country altogether.

b. If food is scarce and people are dying at an alarming rate, that is a starvation issue. Our crop selection must feature the fastest-growing crops, so the greatest possible number of lives can be saved.

c. If food sources exist but not in sufficient supply, and/or the local economy cannot sustain farms and farmers, we have a multiple-needs situation. A combination of supporting food systems and community development assistance is required.

The Politics of Food

Let us be clear that WHT will never - ever - become a political organization.

Our mission is growing food and feeding people, NOT changing the political mindset, intervening in local governments, or trying to change the community structure in our service areas.

Suffice it to say that WHT will not continue to serve a community if it is not benefitting the local people on a nutritional basis. If we become the problem rather than the solution, we must simply leave. We are hoping to interface with many of the existing social / political charities and human welfare organizations which have developed the necessary skills and track record to intervene in the management of local communities and governments. We do not want to duplicate their efforts or re-invent the wheel. WHT provides a sustainable source of food where it is critically needed; that is our mission and our reason for being.

That being said, let us look at the potential crops we can grow in our various growing facilities.

Choosing The Right Food To Grow for The Communities We Serve

The people in every WHT community will have very strong opinions of what they want to eat. At first, they will take what is given and be glad for it. But as health is restored, personal preferences will prevail. And that is a good thing; as anyone who works in a senior center or geriatric unit of a hospital will tell you, once people start complaining about the food they are generally on a clear path to recovery. In other words, they're feeling good enough to know what they prefer and what maximizes their enjoyment at mealtime.

The beauty of the WHT solution is that we can provide the necessary facilities to grow ANY type of food. If it grows in the ground, we can create the environment for it to grow and prosper - AND we can enlist the expertise of the leading professionals who have devoted their life to growing that specific crop. Often, we will find all the expertise we need right in the village we are serving.

Here is a broad overview of the types of crops we can hope to produce in WHT growing facilities:

Vegetables

There are six major categories of vegetables, five of which will be of primary concern to WHT.

1. Leafy and salad vegetables
These include lettuce, spinach, kale, watercress, all types of greens, etc.

2. Fruiting and flowering vegetables
Here we have tomatoes, squash, eggplant, peppers, pumpkin, cucumbers, etc.

3. Podded vegetables
This category includes all types of beans, peas, lentils, rice, peanuts, and many others.

4. Bulb and stem vegetables
This category includes onion, garlic, asparagus, celery, radishes, etc.

5. Root and tuberous vegetables
Here we have carrots, potatoes, parsnips, turnips, rutabagas, yams, etc.

6. Sea vegetables
This category of vegetables will likely not come into play with WHT, but we are including it to be thorough. This category includes sea grapes, sea lettuce, carola, mozuku, etc. - mostly vegetables consumed in seaside communities, especially in Asia.

In addition to these vegetables, we have fruit trees to consider, as well as plants with edible leaves and root vegetables.

Crop Selection

Here is a basic overview of the types of crops we believe can be grown in each of our two building categories.

Full-Protection / Sealed Greenhouses
- Tomatoes
- Cucumbers
- Lettuce
- Squash
- Green Beans

Limited-Protection Growing Facilities (Hot Houses)
- Potatoes & Sweet Potatoes
- Carrots
- Peanuts
- Radishes
- Chickpeas
- Soybeans
- Peppers
- Onions

We believe that peanuts will be an important crop in every WHT facility. This is because peanuts are a very versatile crop - one simply needs to view the body of work of George Washington Carver to sense its versatility. While most of Dr. Carver's research and techniques were lost, some of his more basic findings have been applied to commercial production. Most notable is the ability to press cooking oil out of peanuts. Fried foods, while decried by most of the nutrition community, remain the #1 preference around the world.

As the WHT communities begin to prosper and day-to-day nutrition takes the place of starvation prevention, the local people will want to return to their native recipes - many of which will call for frying. Peanut oil is considered to be one of the pre-eminent oils for healthy frying, so producing it in quantity in the WHT communities will be vital.

The World is Chock-Full of Growing Expertise

It is very important to note that a tremendous amount of knowledge exists in growing vegetables in greenhouses and hot houses. Agricultural colleges and universities have been perfecting the art of greenhouse growing for years, and of course the commercial greenhouses have been perfecting their processes for centuries. For example, Mississippi State University has established the "bible" of tomato growing. It can be found at:

http://msucares.com/pubs/publications/p1828.htm

This is just one example of the scope and depth of knowledge that is available today. Our goal at WHT is to enlist not only the education community, but the commercial growing community as well, in our quest to reach maximum crop output in the shortest possible timeframe.

A world of choices for diverse climates and cultures

As noted earlier, WHT can alter the variety of vegetables to suit local tastes and preferences, as well as to match the specific climate of any region in the world. We are not limited to commercial strains of vegetables that are best suited to one specific locale. **The Seed Savers Exchange** (www.seedsavers.org) has been collecting, preserving and expanding the distribution of heirloom seeds since 1975.

Quoting from their website: "Seed Savers Exchange is a non-profit, member supported organization that saves and shares the heirloom seeds of our garden heritage, forming a living legacy that can be passed down through generations. Our loyal SSE members have distributed an estimated 1 million samples of rare garden seeds since our founding nearly 35 years ago. Those seeds now are widely used by seed companies, small farmers supplying local and regional markets, chefs and home gardeners and cooks, alike."

Why is the preservation of these diverse plant varieties important? It is precisely because nature has pre-engineered specific traits into these varieties, allowing them to thrive in diverse conditions. Many of these plant varieties are threatened with extinction due to the fragile nature of their fruit; in today's economy, if the fruit (output of the plant) cannot travel well or does not have a long shelf-life, it is incompatible with the needs of the commercial marketplace, so it is not widely grown. If these varieties are no longer cultivated, their seeds - and their specific contributions to the food chain - could be lost forever.

Again, from the Seed Savers Exchange website: "The genetic diversity of the world's food crops is eroding at an unprecedented and accelerating rate. The vegetables and fruits currently being lost are the result of thousands of years of adaptation and selection in diverse ecological niches around the world. Each variety is genetically unique and has developed resistance to the diseases and pests with which it evolved. Plant breeders use the old varieties to breed resistance into modern crops that are constantly being attacked by rapidly evolving diseases and pests. Without these infusions of genetic diversity, food production is at risk from epidemics and infestations."

The potential loss of plant varieties - which have developed over tens of thousands - and perhaps millions of years - could be devastating to the balance of the natural food chain as we know it. Again, from the Seed Savers Exchange website:

"Just how dangerous is genetic erosion? The late Jack Harlan, world renowned plant collector who wrote the classic "Crops and Man" while Professor of Plant Genetics at University of Illinois at Urbana, has written: "These resources stand between us and catastrophic starvation on a scale we cannot imagine. In a very real sense, the future of the human race rides on these materials. The line between abundance and disaster is becoming thinner and thinner, and the public is unaware and unconcerned. Must we wait for disaster to be real before we are heard? Will people listen only after it is too late?"

WHT hopes to work closely with the Seed Savers Exchange organization as we build our implementation plans. By testing a wide range of crop varieties in each of our WHT installations, we can determine which varieties are capable of producing the greatest output of food in the shortest possible timeframe - as well as which will be most resistant to the local diseases and pests.

Drought-Resistant Crops for Desolate Areas

As you can see from the prior discussion, selection of the proper seeds will be very important to the long-term success of WHT installations around the world. Even more important to the viability and long-term success of these installations is crop selection. A crop that grows well in Nebraska may not perform well in Ghana. Similarly, a crop that grows abundantly in Ghana may not survive here in the states.

It will be important to select crops that are needed in the developing countries, rather than crops that we believe they need. In other words, growing the largest possible quantity of green beans in Ethiopia will be meaningless if the residents of Ethiopia cannot tolerate green beans as a food. The foods that are traditionally served in a nation are the foods that they inevitably want on their plates. They will tolerate some variation when starvation exists, but eventually they will want to go back to what they know.

Nature has already made many of these crop selection decisions for us. The crops that grow naturally in a country, (or grew there naturally before the breakdown of the natural food chain by climate change or human intervention), can still grow there. We simply have to promote their growth and cultivation in a controlled environment. Some areas such as jungle zones will favor high-humidity plants, while others will favor drought-resistant plants. It is the installations in these desert-like zones that will require the greatest effort and attention to detail in crop selection, due to the lack of water.

One crop that survives remarkably well in water-deprived areas is **Pigeon Peas**. Pigeon peas are both a food crop (dried peas, flour, or green vegetable peas) and a forage/cover crop. The dried peas may be sprouted briefly, then cooked, for a flavor different from the green or dried peas. Sprouting also enhances the digestability of dried pigeon peas via the reduction of indigestible sugars that would otherwise remain in the cooked dried peas.

In India, split pigeon peas (toor dal) are one of the most popular "pulses" - along with chickpeas (chana), urad and mung. It is also called 'tuvara parippu' in Kerala. In south India a popular dish called "sambhar" is made with this. Dal is also made with pigeon peas. Pulses, such as beans, lentils and chickpeas, are the "meat" of India – the main source of protein for most of its 1 billion people. Flour can be made out of many of these pulses, which can be used to cook nutritious foods and snack items.

According to the U.S. Department of Agriculture FAS Information Division website[5], "throughout India, peas are cooked and eaten as snack foods or used as fillers in traditional snacks such as samosas. Split yellow peas and pea flour are increasingly being blended with similar looking, but more expensive, split chickpeas and flour. Lentils are generally served along with rice as dal. Dal, garnished with onions and spices, is an indispensable entree in roadside dhabas (quick, cheap eateries). Dal also is found on menus of five-star hotels."

In some places, such as the Dominican Republic and Hawaii, pigeon peas

[5] http://www.fas.usda.gov/info/agexporter/2000/Apr/uspulses.htm

are grown for canning. On the Caribbean Island of Puerto Rico, rice and green pigeon peas are together considered the main traditional food, served as a representative Puerto Rican cuisine in many food festivals around the world. For example, it garnered great reviews in <u>The Taste of Chicago 2007</u>, an annual food festival.

The woody stems of pigeon peas are used as firewood, fencing and thatch. In Thailand, pigeon peas are grown as a host for scale insects which produce lac, a key ingredient in shellac and varnish.

In most areas, pigeon peas are grown in association with other row crops such as sorghum, pearl millet, or maize. Pigeon peas can be of a perennial type, in which the crop can last 3-5 years (although the seed yield drops considerably after the first two years), or an annual type more suitable for grain production.

The crop is cultivated on marginal land by resource-poor farmers, who commonly grow traditional medium and long duration (5-11 months) landraces. Short duration pigeon peas (3-4 months) suitable for multiple cropping have recently been developed. The use of fertilizers, weeding, irrigation, and pesticides have historically been minimal, so present yield levels are low (average = 700 kg/hac). Greater attention is now being given to managing the crop due to high demand and rising crop value.

Pigeon peas are very drought resistant and can be grown in areas with less than 650 mm annual rainfall. World production of pigeon peas is estimated at 46,000 km. About 82% of this is grown in India. These days it is the most essential ingredient of animal feed used in West Africa, most especially in Nigeria where it is also grown. As chickens, cows, goats and other animals are added to the WHT community mix, pigeon peas can become a vital source of animal food.

A similar 'pulse' grown here in the U.S. is called Pardina. According to Pete Johnstone, president and CEO of Spokane Seed Company, Pardina is "the smallest, and currently the least expensive lentil grown on the planet." Pardina differs from most lentils. It is grey in color, and a little smaller than a an average lentil. Yet because this pulse is easy to grow and produces highly-nutritious peas in large quantities, it could be an excellent addition to the WHT growing facilities.

Chapter 24 - Sprouts: Quick Food for the Neediest of Areas

In areas with widespread starvation, it will be important to grow the greatest amount of edible food in the shortest possible time frame. Nature's fastest-growing food is sprouts; the shoots that grow from wetted seeds. According to Wikipedia, sprouting is the practice of soaking, draining and then rinsing seeds at regular intervals until they germinate, or sprout. This process can be completed in as few as 3 days, making sprouts an ideal solution to feeding people quickly in the areas of greatest need.

One of the most common sprouts is that of the mung bean (Vigna radiata); another common sprout is the Kala Chana & alfalfa sprout and the barley sprout.

Other seeds that can be sprouted include adzuki bean, almond, amaranth, annatto seed, anise seed, arugula, basil, brown rice, navy bean, pinto bean, lima bean, broccoli, buckwheat, cabbage, canola seed, caragana, cauliflower, celery, chia seed, chickpeas, chives, cilantro (coriander, dhania), clover, cress, dill, fennel, fenugreek, flax seed, garlic, hemp seed, kale, kamut, kat, leek, green lentils, lupins, pearl millet, mizuna, mustard, oats, onion, black-eyed peas, green peas, pigeon peas, snow peas, peanut, psyllium, pumpkin, quinoa, radish, rye, sesame, soybean, spelt, sunflower, tatsoi, triticale, watercress, and wheat berries.

Sprouting is also applied on a large scale to barley as a part of the malting process. Malted barley is an important ingredient in beer and is used in huge quantities.

However, many sprouts are, in fact, toxic when eaten, like kidney beans.

Some sprouts can be cooked to remove the toxin, while others will be toxic either way and should be avoided. So before eating any varieties, it is advisable to find out if that species is edible as a sprout.

With all seeds, care should be taken that they are intended for sprouting or human consumption rather than sowing. Seeds intended for sowing may be treated with chemical dressings. Several countries, such as New Zealand, also require that some varieties of edible seed be heat-treated, thus making them impossible to sprout.

Edible Food in As Little as 3 to 5 Days

To sprout seeds, the seeds are moistened, and then left at room temperature (between 13 and 21 degrees Celsius) in a sprouting vessel. Many different types of vessels can be used. One type is a simple glass jar with a piece of cloth secured over its rim. 'Tiered' clear plastic sprouters are commercially available, allowing a number of "crops" to be grown simultaneously. By staggering sowings, a constant supply of young sprouts can be ensured. Any vessel used for sprouting must allow water to drain from it, because sprouts that sit in water will rot quickly. The seeds will swell and begin germinating within a day or two.

Sprouts are rinsed as little as twice a day, but possibly three or four times a day in hotter climates, to prevent them from souring. Each seed has its own ideal sprouting time. Depending on which seed is used, after three to five days they will have grown to two or three inches in length and will be suitable for consumption. If left longer they will begin to develop leaves, and are then known as baby greens. A popular baby green is sunflower after 7-10 days. The growth process of any sprout can be slowed or halted by refrigerating until needed.

Common causes for sprouts to become inedible:
- *Seeds are allowed to dry out*
- *Seeds are left in standing water*
- *Temperature is high or too low*
- *Insufficient rinsing*
- *Dirty equipment*
- *Insufficient air flow*
- *Contaminated source of water*
- *Poor rate of germination of seed*

Sprouter

The problems described above are easily solved by an automatic sprouter that mists and drains the sprouts at regular intervals. To control temperature, in the winter a warming blanket can be placed under the sprouter, and in the summer small fans in the lid if it's very hot and humid. We anticipate that a contributing WHT engineer can design a simplified sprouter machine that has these needed features. The fans can be powered by solar panels; the water irrigation can be powered by gravity and simple timers. Where there is a will, there is a way, and an easy-to-use automated sprouter machine could be the key to growing mass quantities of sprouts to easily feed a starving community.

Chapter 25 - Bread: The Cornerstone of Life

Bread is a staple of life. It will be critical for WHT to find the proper crops, growing methodology, ingredients, and recipes to bake bread. Bread is at the core of nutrition in every country of the world. The obvious obstacle is that growing wheat is not always easy, especially in arid climates and regions with poor soil conditions. There are various breads that can be made without wheat, a classic example being Essene bread.

Typically made with wheat sprouts, wheat kernels, chickpeas, and lentils, Essene bread is thought to be the manna that the tribes of Israel lived on during their trek from Egypt to the Promised Land. An ancient recipe for this flourless bread appears in the first century Aramaic manuscript entitled *The Essene Gospel of Peace*. It is also said that this bread was eaten by cavemen in the prehistoric era, who baked wafers made from a grain-water paste on sun-heated stones. If the cavemen could master this recipe in primitive conditions, surely we in the 21st century can master a recipe to feed the hungry throughout the world!

The key to making Essene bread is wheat sprouts. Once you have an active, replenishing supply of wheat kernels, you can grow sprouts quickly and make bread indefinitely. The key will be in germinating an ongoing supply of wheat kernels - and this is a question I will leave in the hands of the biologists and farmers. Will we be able to grow and harvest wheat in a controlled environment? If so, much of the challenge in nourishing the hungry in an adverse environment will have been solved.

A great source for sprout information is run by a consultant to WHT, Isabell Shipard. Her site is found at http://www.herbsarespecial.com.au. Isabell operates an herb farm in Nambour, Queensland, Australia. Her knowledge of growing and using herbs as culinary delights, alternative medicines and herbal remedies has been featured on media around the world, including a 10-year guest role on the ABC Radio Coast FM "Herb of the Week" show.

According to Shipard, botanists have identified almost 30,000 species and developed varieties of wheat. Surely we can find one of these that can be grown in our WHT facilities. But wheat is not the only plant whose kernels can be turned into flour. There are many, many plants and seeds that can be made into flour, including the following, as posted on Wikipedia:

- **Amaranth flour** is a flour produced from ground Amaranth grain. It was commonly used in pre-Columbian meso-American cuisine. It is becoming more and more available in speciality food shops.

- **Atta flour** is a whole-grain wheat flour important in Indian and Pakistani cuisine, used for a range of breads such as roti, naan and chapati.

- **Bean flour** is a flour produced from pulverized dried or ripe beans.

- **Brown rice flour** is of great importance in Southeast Asian cuisine. Also, edible rice paper can be made from it. Most rice flour is made from white rice, thus is essentially a pure starch, but whole-grain brown rice flour is commercially available.

- **Buckwheat flour** is used as an ingredient in many pancakes in the United States. In Japan, it is used to make a popular noodle called Soba. In Russia, buckwheat flour is added to the batter for pancakes called blinis which are frequently eaten with caviar. Buckwheat flour is also used to make crêpes bretonnes in Brittany.

- **Nut flours** are grated from oily nuts - most commonly almonds and hazelnuts - and are used instead of or in addition to wheat flour to produce more dry and flavorful pastries and cakes. Cakes made with nut flours are usually called tortes and most originated in Central Europe, in countries such as Hungary and Austria.

- **Chestnut flour** is popular in Corsica, the Périgord and Lunigiana for breads, cakes and pastas. It is the original ingredient for "polenta", still used as such in Corsica and other Mediterranean locations. Chestnut bread keeps fresh for as long as two weeks. In other parts of Italy it is mainly used for desserts.

- **Chickpea flour** (also known as gram flour or besan) is of great importance in Indian cuisine, and in Italy, where it is used for the Ligurian farinata.

- **Chuño flour** made from dried potatoes in various countries of South America.

- **Corn (maize) flour** is popular in the Southern and Southwestern US, Mexico, South America, and Punjab regions of India and Pakistan. Coarse whole-grain corn flour is usually called corn meal. Corn meal that has been bleached with lye is called masa harina and is used to make tortillas and tamales in Mexican cooking.

- **Peasemeal or pea flour** is a flour produced from roasted and pulverized yellow field peas.

- **Rye flour** is used to bake the traditional sourdough breads of Germany and Scandinavia. Most rye breads use a mix of rye and wheat flours because rye does not produce gluten. Pumpernickel bread is usually made exclusively of rye, and contains a mixture of rye flour and rye meal.

- **Tapioca flour**, produced from the root of the cassava plant, is used to make breads, pancakes, tapioca pudding, a savory porridge called fufu in Africa, and is used as a starch.

- **Teff flour** is made from the grain teff, and is of considerable importance in eastern Africa (particularly around the horn of Africa). Notably, it is the chief ingredient in the bread "injera", an important component of Ethiopian cuisine.

- **Other rare flours** are made from Spelt (also called Dinkel wheat), Indian Fig, Arrowroot, Sacred Lotus, Kudzu (yes, the same Kudzu that is strangling all wildlife throughout the Southern United States), and many other roots and herbs. These specialty flours are often mixed with traditional wheat flour to add flavor or medicinal properties to recipes.

We will entrust experts such as Isabell Shipard to develop the ideal combination of plant selection, output and production methodology to select our 'flour producing' procedures. The world needs bread, and together we can help provide it!

Fruits to Feed a Hungry Planet

Our plant selection in WHT installations will not be limited to vegetables; we will be growing fruits, as well! Again, selecting the proper fruits to grow will be left to the experts. One of the top organizations in this field is The California Rare Fruit Growers, Inc., http://www.crfg.org. According to their website, CRFG is a "non-profit educational organization devoted to providing information to our members and the public on (primarily) tree crop culture." Their site lists over 1,000 fruits of the world by their common names, and features a list of over 700 individual fruits arranged by scientific name with temperature limits and information on soil conditions.

We believe that our 9-grid macro farming solution could support large-scale orchards throughout our worldwide WHT installations. It is our goal to have experts such as CRFG play a major role in crop selection, installation and management of these orchards.

Chapter 26 - Other Growing Methods: Hydroponics

Hydroponics (from the Greek words hydro (water) and ponos (labor) is a method of growing plants using mineral nutrient solutions, without soil. Terrestrial plants may be grown with their roots in the mineral nutrient solution only or in an inert medium, such as perlite, gravel, or mineral wool. Hardly a new phenomenon, the study was introduced in a 1627 book by Sir Francis Bacon, <u>Sylva Sylvarum</u>, published a year after his death.

The two chief merits of the soilless cultivation of plants are:

1. *Much higher crop yields than soil-based growing.*
2. *The fact that hydroponics can be used in places where ordinary agriculture or gardening is impossible.*

An early 20th century advocate of hydroponics was Professor William Frederick Gericke of the University of California at Berkeley. In 1929, Gericke began publicly promoting that solution culture be used for agricultural crop production. He created a sensation by growing tomato vines <u>*twenty-five feet high*</u> in his back yard in mineral nutrient solutions rather than soil. Do you think the hungry people of the world could benefit from having 25-feet high tomato plants growing in their communities?

One would initially think that water-based growing would require significantly MORE water than traditional soil-based growing methods. But in fact:

- Hydroponics saves an incredible amount of water; it uses as little as 1/20 the amount of water as traditional farming methods to produce the same amount of food.

- Using hydroponics, plants absorb essential mineral nutrients that manifest themselves as vitamins and minerals in the food product. The yield is nutritious, healthy food that can often grow much faster than in soil.

The largest commercial hydroponics facility in the world is Eurofresh Farms in Willcox, Arizona, which sold 125 million pounds of tomatoes in 2005. Eurofresh has 318 acres (1.29 km2) under glass and represents about a third of the commercial hydroponic greenhouse area in the U.S. Eurofresh does not consider its tomatoes organic, but they are pesticide-free. They are grown in rockwool with top irrigation.

Benefits of Hydroponics

According to the website www.PlantCare.com, the principal benefits of soilless growing include:

- *Complete control over nutrient balance*
- *pH and nutrient levels are simple to measure and maintain*
- *Significant reduction of soil pests and diseases*
- *Greater spacing efficiency due to smaller roots*
- *Concentrated feeding reduces water waste*

In addition, the website states that "plants expend a great deal of energy growing root systems so they can search the soil for the water and nutrients they need to survive. By providing constant and readily available nutrition, hydroponics allows plants to grow up to 50% faster than they do in soil."

This one benefit alone - increased speed of plant growth - could be the determining factor in making hydroponics our #1 choice for growing methodologies in all WHT installations.

Chapter 27 - Fertilization, Pesticides and Pollination

Fertilization

Another key question that will arise is, how do we fertilize the plants, and how do we prevent infestation from local predators? In the early phases of development, we propose to ship in the fertilizer and pesticide supplies from the U.S. Developing a more localized solution will require time and investment. We discussed one possible solution in Chapter 16, using the by-product of our methane gas production operation as fertilizer. Just how effective is it? Again, quoting from The Mother Earth News Jan/Feb 1974 edition, *"Mother's Methane Maker:"*

"We had heard that the spent slurry taken from a digester would be rich in nitrogen ... but we weren't prepared for what happened when we dumped the composted waste on a bare patch of ground. The digested slurry actually soaked into the soil faster than plain water! The earth was that "hungry" for it. Furthermore, the particular spot of land (where it was applied) was bare because dad had scraped off all its topsoil approximately 18 or 20 years before. Nothing had grown there since. But—now get this!—grass did start to grow on that same barren area two weeks after we doused it with the composted manure. A miraculous cure indeed ... and it impressed the heck out of us."

Pesticides

Regarding pesticides, there are many natural deterrents to using chemicals to control bugs. For example, planting certain flowers among the food crops can deter many local bugs; they hate the smell of the flowers, so they stay away from the crops. There are many natural deterrents that can ward off predators, and we will rely on the botanists to maximize this approach. There will be a need for chemical deterrents as well, and these will be sourced locally or shipped in to support the local WHT facilities.

Pollination

Another key factor in any growing facility will be pollination. How will we fertilize the plants in a controlled, indoor environment. Again, we will leave it to the experts on the Botany Team to select the appropriate germination method for each installation. Greenhouse production of vegetables has been in practice for hundreds if not thousands of years, so there is no need to reinvent the wheel here, either.

As every high school student learns, "Pollination is the process by which pollen is transferred in plants, thereby enabling fertilization and sexual reproduction," according to Wikipedia. There are two types of pollination:

Abiotic - i.e., no involvement from other organizations is required. The most common form, anemophily, is pollination by wind.

Biotic - pollination that requires pollinators: organisms that carry or move the pollen grains from the anther to the receptive part of the carpel or pistil. There are roughly 200,000 varieties of animal pollinators in the wild, most of which are insects.

- **Entomophily** is pollination by insects, and often occurs on plants that have developed colored petals and a strong scent to attract insects such as, bees, wasps and occasionally ants, beetles, moths and butterflies, and flies.
- **Zoophily** is pollination by vertebrates such as birds and bats, particularly hummingbirds, sunbirds, spiderhunters, honeyeaters, and fruit bats.

Abiotic pollination in a greenhouse environment is often facilitated through the use of electric vibrators, mist blowers, striking the plant's support wires, and even through the use of electric toothbrushes.

Biotic pollination is often achieved through the use of honeybees and flying insects such as lady bugs.

An excellent resource for pollination requirements by crop is found at the website http://www.pollinator.com.

With the rapid changes in our global climate and natural resources, pollination is not a topic that should be taken lightly. According to the website for **The North American Pollinator Protection Campaign** and

The Pollinator Partnership (http://www.pollinator.org), the natural presence of pollinators in our world is in jeopardy.

According to the organization's web site, "At least 80% of our world's crop plant species require pollination. Estimates as high as one out of every third bite of food comes to us through the work of animal pollinators. Birds, bees, butterflies, and also bats, beetles and even mosquitoes are among the myriad creatures which transfer pollen between seed plants. This function is vital for plant reproduction and food production.

Declines in the health and population of pollinators in North America and globally pose what could be a significant threat to the integrity of biodiversity, to global food webs, and to human health. A number of pollinator species are at risk."

We have all heard the story of bee colonies mysteriously dying, and farmers paying to 'rent' colonies of bees to populate their crops. It is our hope that WHT facilities can help propagate honey bee populations in our facilities to help mitigate these declines.

Chapter 28 - Feed The Hungry

It would be convenient to believe that once the food is grown, people will simply distribute the food evenly among them and live in harmony. But the reality is that food equals power in an environment where sufficient food supplies do not exist. The criminal element will quickly seek to take control of the food-growing process and facilities, in order to gain political control over the people. WHT cannot prevent this. But we CAN seek to implement controls over:

- *How the food is grown and stored.*
- *How the food is prepared and served.*
- *How the local people and leaders are established as leaders of the WHT facilities.*
- *How the WHT facility interfaces with local farmers and helps to maintain their economic viability*

Our goal is to turn complete control of the WHT facilities over to local leaders. It will be up to these leaders and their local and national government to deal with the regional politics and policing issues. But WHT can help in their control of the facilities by establishing a set of ground rules by which the facility is *intended* to operate. We will have little control over how the facility is *actually* operated once we have turned over control to the local leaders.

Food Distribution

Vegetables are truly amazing in that they feature their own built-in freshness seal; a tomato can stay edible for several weeks if kept out of the sun and away from moisture. Carrots have a built-in cover that is typically shaved off before eating. Corn has a multi-layer wrapper that grows naturally to protect the kernels inside. Every fruit and vegetable on earth has its own protective layer that enables it to remain edible for weeks or even months after harvesting. This means that the food that is grown in a WHT greenhouse can be transported to other parts of the country to help solve hunger in locations far removed from our installations. It also means that we can expand our operations in one convenient locale and spread the wealth to communities far removed from our growing facilities. The net result: We don't have to build facilities in every community of need; we simply need to establish a regional food distribution system if none exists.

Food Preparation and Cooking

A great documentary recently aired on the Documentary Channel about the use of solar cookers in Africa. Because firewood is in such high demand but short supply, Africans often have to do without cooking their food. As a solution, someone created an ingenious cardboard and foil device that is low cost, yet efficiently harnesses the power of the sun to cook food. The same unit is also used to boil water and disinfect it. These inexpensive solar cookers are gaining popularity in Africa because they allow the citizens to prepare better and more diverse meals.

We propose the development of a more permanent and large-scale cooking facility using multiple versions of this same device. Imagine the power of being able to cook for large quantities of people in a facility that uses no fuel for cooking. Granted, the facility can only be used on days when it is sunny. But if the number of sunny days constitutes 2/3 of the year, the commissary will have a free and abundant source of cooking power for the vast majority of the year. On the days that it is cloudy or rainy, the kitchen stove can be fueled using the methane gas option discussed in Chapter 16 of this book.

These solar ovens will be permanent fixtures, so they can likely be built entirely out of metal, or built of brick with metal reflecting panels that collect the sun. This will be up to the engineers to decide.

Commercial-size solar ovens have been developed, and are readily available today. For an example, visit the website of a company called "Reflections" based in Rough & Ready, California, http://www.solarovens.net and scroll to the bottom of the page. The company manufactures a model called the "Villager Solar Oven", which they state can cook over 1,200 meals per day or bake hundreds of loaves of bread. With a top dimension of 25.8 square feet, this immense solar cooker could cook enough food to feed an entire village. According to the company's website, "The Villager Solar Oven - Sun Oven is designed for large-scale feeding situations that require cooking great volumes of food quickly with just the power of the Sun. Even though it is called an oven, enormous quantities of food can be boiled, steamed or baked at cooking temperatures of 500° F / 260° C with no fuel costs."

The company has even developed an invention to maximize the efficiency of their solar cookers. Called the "Solar Oven Tracker", this device "permits unattended operation all day long. The solar oven tracker follows the path of the sun and rotates your solar oven through the day. Since the oven is always properly adjusted at the right angle to achieve the highest possible temperature, this allows for faster cooking without manually adjusting your oven as the sun moves across the sky. Simply place your Solar Oven on the lazy susan style sturdy handmade painted plywood platform, which is self powered by a small solar panel that directly drives a small solar powered motor connected to the wheels of the platform," according to the company's website.

In other words, a self-powered device exists today that can maximize the efficiency of a huge commercial solar cooker, so no manpower or expertise is needed out in the field to mass produce meals for a hungry village. In theory, 2 or 3 of these huge devices could cook all of the food needed for a community of several thousand residents. There will be NO cost for fuel, NO recurring expense, and NO pollution caused by burning wood or fossil fuel. The technology is readily available, so again - we do not have to reinvent the wheel. We can use these massive solar cookers to cook all of the food needed at any WHT installation around the world - regardless of whether there is electricity, natural gas, or other conventional fuel source available at the site.

These same solar cookers can also be used to boil water, killing the bacteria and pathogens that can lead to illness or death.

Water sanitation and health is a major concern of the World Health Organization (http://www.who.int). Water-borne pathogens can cause typhoid fever, hepatitis A and E, cholera, and dysentery, among others, all major killers in underdeveloped nations. Boiling water to kill these pathogens is much more effective and safe than adding chemicals, as well as being a totally natural solution to a huge and growing health problem.

We believe that these large-scale commercial solar cookers could be used to boil the drinking water for entire communities in these remote areas. This one step alone could go a long way to improving the health and life expectancy of people in the poorest areas of the world.

Dietary Concerns

Perhaps the most important aspect of feeding a community is maintaining a nutritional balance in the citizen's diets. WHT will certainly need nutritionists on staff, so the crops we produce will promote a healthy and complete diet. As previously discussed, the immediate need will be to stave off hunger, which will be followed in phases by increasing levels of diversity and complexity in the food output. We believe that the addition of poultry and cattle to produce meat, eggs and milk will be critical to the program's success. In taking this position, we are prepared to face public outcry from vegetarians and animal rights activists. However, our goal is not to irritate these individuals and groups; our goal is to feed people. And it is a well-known fact that poultry, dairy products, eggs and meat are exceptional sources of nutrition for humans.

Mixed farming has benefits to the entire community as well. According to Keith Addison of the organization "Journey to Forever" (http://journeytoforever.org), "Mixed farming is best. Nature never tries to raise crops without animals, and the more species in attendance the better. This doesn't mean extra management problems, it means increased biodiversity - which works in your favor in many ways, meaning fewer management problems. Fewer pests, less disease, higher yields, fertile soil, a healthy farm, and all your eggs in many different baskets."

This innovative organization is using the internet to link schools and communities around the world to confront a wide range of environmental issues. Their stated goal is to "help people fight poverty and hunger, and to help sustain the environment we all must share." The group is involved in environmental and rural development issues, and is operating a traveling program starting in Hong Kong and traveling through 26 countries in Asia and Africa to Cape Town, South Africa.

According to its website, this excursion will "take us away from the cities and populated districts to remote and inaccessible areas (usually also the least developed and poorest areas), where we'll be studying and reporting on environmental conditions and working for local NGOs on rural development projects in local communities. The focus will be on trees, soil and water, sustainable farming, sustainable technology, and family nutrition[6]."

Addressing the Local Food Preferences

One of the questions that will inevitably come up is, "what if the locals want to grow their own favorite foods, and not tomatoes, squash, cucumbers, or whatever WHT has decided is best for them?" And the answer is, GREAT! Let the local preferences dictate what is grown, and let's learn from their experiences how best to grow those plants.

For example, let's say that a village in Afghanistan loves to put mint leaves in their tea - but mint leaves are a very costly, precious commodity there. This could be caused by high temperatures or shortage of water; whatever the reason, the locals cannot get enough mint leaves. In such a case, WHT will simply set another growing facility dedicated exclusively to mint leaf production with a cost of practically nothing, since our primary building supplies are made from trash. How much additional plastic will we need to build another greenhouse in a remote village 300 miles outside of Kandahar? Well, about as much waste plastic as the city of Passaic, New Jersey will produce between - say, 10 a.m. this morning and 3 p.m. You get the idea? We can produce as many greenhouses as the world needs, for whatever the world needs, because we've got a practically unlimited supply of building materials!

---

[6] *Our thanks and best wishes to Keith Addison and his team from "Journey to Forever", who sent his approval to quote from his current location in KYOTO Pref., Japan.*

Controlling the Food Distribution

An issue that will certainly be raised is the equality of food distribution - who gets the right to eat, and who must do without? It will be virtually impossible to feed every person in need, every day. Some food that is not yet ready for consumption must remain on the vine so it can develop to meet tomorrow's needs - even if hungry people are in line outside of the greenhouse. Is this 'playing God'? Is this denying people the right to live, when their lives might potentially be saved by eating the semi-ripe fruits? These are questions to be debated. We must think of the long-term success of the facility; if the entire plant inventory is depleted, there will be no food available for tomorrow's needs.

The answer in the grand scheme of things is to add more greenhouses to insure a reliable and ongoing supply of food. By rotating the growing schedule, we can assure a steady and ever-present source of food in the relief community. This will require strong management - and strong locks on the doors. You've heard the saying, 'good fences make good neighbors.' In this case, good security protection on the greenhouses will make for a good and reliable food supply.

Chapter 29 - Medical Needs in Remote Villages

There is always a shortage of medicine in poor countries, and people die every day for lack of basic medicines and remedies. Many times, the core components of these medicines are found in simple plants. We can grow these plants in our greenhouses, so the local doctors have access to herbs that can either reduce the symptoms of their patients or cure them of their illnesses. Granted, it would be far better for these doctors to have access to professionally manufactured drugs in a limitless supply; but in a world where budgets are shrinking and charitable donations are declining rapidly, wouldn't it be better to have *some* remedies rather than *none*?

Here are just a few of the plants that can be grown at WHT installations and the ailments they treat:

Species	Common Name	Indication
Allium sativum	Garlic	Antibiotic (in vitro) / stops infection
Artemisia annua L.	Sweet sagewort	Help to prevent the development of parasite resistance. Also has anti-malarial properties, and has anti-cancer properties
Citrus aurantium ssp. Bergamia	Bergamot orange	Useful in the treatment of malaria
Crataegus spp. L.	Hawthorn	Treatment of nervous tension
Digitalis lanata	Digitalis, Balkan Foxglove	Antiarrhythmic agent and inotrope
Hydrastis C anadensis	Goldenseal	Antimicrobial agent
Marrubium vulgare	Horehound	Expectorant
Chamomilla recutita	Chamomile	Relaxant/Calmative
Mentha x piperita	Peppermint	Irritable Bowel Syndrome/Peristalsis
Nepeta cataria	Catnip	Soothes coughs
Gymnema sylvestre	Gymnema	Diabetes, stomach ailments, constipation, water retention, and liver disease.
Phytolacca spp.	Pokeweed	External: treatment of acne. Internal: treatment of tonsilitis
Plantago spp.	Plantain and Psyllium	Astringent
Symphytum officinale	Comfrey	Mends broken bones / stops infection

Tanacetum parthenium	Feverfew	Relieves migraine headaches, helps fevers and chills
Taraxacum officinale	Dandelion	Relieves digestive disorders
Tilia spp.	Lime Blossom	Sedative
Verbascum Thapsus	Mullein	Boosts the immune system, antispasmodic, diuretic, anodyne, and demulcent. Used to treat coughs, (protracted) colds, hemoptysis, catarrh, dysentery, diarrhea and as a general tonic (like ginseng) to boost the immune system

It is also important to consider the fact that the world relied on plants and herbs as its ONLY source of medicinal remedies prior to the development of modern medicine in the last 100 to 200 years.

India has used herbs as medicine since the dawn of man. In traditional Indian Ayurvedic medicine, vegetable drugs are at the core of a regimen of holistic treatment which includes the use of herbs, massage, yoga and exercise in the treatment of ailments. In India, over 100 colleges offer degrees in traditional Ayurvedic medicine.

To this day, the Chinese rely on 50 basic herbs to create their medicines, and these are not 'experimental' medical procedures: they have been in daily practice for centuries in China.

In fact, one of the earliest Chinese manuals on pharmacology, the <u>Shennong Bencao Jing</u> (*Shennong Emperor's Classic of Materia Medica*), lists some 365 medicines of which 252 are herbs. The book dates back to the 1st century C.E. Han dynasty. Earlier literature included lists of prescriptions for specific ailments, exemplified by a manuscript, "<u>Recipes for 52 Ailments</u>", found in the Mawangdui tomb, sealed in 168 B.C. These prescriptions are nothing more than herbs which are ground up, mixed with other ingredients, and served as a type of herbal 'cocktail'.

(If this brings to mind a picture of America's perennial teenager Jack LaLanne drinking an herb & vegetable concoction ground up in his juicer machine, there may be a logical connection. Jack was 95 years young and still strong as a mule at the time of this writing...)

From Wikipedia: "Herbology is one of the more important modalities utilized in traditional Chinese medicine (TCM). Each herbal medicine prescription is a cocktail of many herbs tailored to the individual patient. One batch of herbs is typically decocted twice over the course of one hour. The practitioner usually designs a remedy using one or two main ingredients that target the illness. Then the practitioner adds many other ingredients to adjust the formula to the patient's yin / yang conditions. Sometimes, ingredients are needed to cancel out toxicity or side-effects of the main ingredients. Some herbs require the use of other ingredients as catalyst or else the brew is ineffective. The latter steps require great experience and knowledge, and make the difference between a good Chinese herbal doctor and an amateur.

Unlike western medications, the balance and interaction of all the ingredients are considered more important than the effect of individual ingredients. A key to success in TCM is the treatment of each patient as an individual."

It is no secret in business communities that the Chinese are expanding their industrial influence and resource mining throughout Africa. As their presence in Africa increases, could not their medicinal knowledge be used to help to treat the sick and dying in these regions? Surely, some in the Western world would balk at this and demand that we utilize only our tested and proven conventional medical methods. But this raises the question: If our approach to medicine is the only one to be considered when attempting to solve the world's medical problems, why haven't we been able to succeed thus far in the poorest regions of the world? Conversely, if we could grow the herbs required to make a serious impact on the health and wellness of the world's massive population, don't we owe it to ourselves - and the sick and dying masses of the world - to consider alternative approaches?

You may ask yourself, what good would it be to grow Chinese herbs in Haiti, Mexico, South America, or deepest Africa, when there are no Chinese herbologists or Indian Ayurvedic practitioners present? The answer: Our goal is to have each WHT facility linked to the web via a solar-cell powered computer, a webcam, and a satellite connection link. With this technology in place, the following could be achieved:

- A Chinese physician in a remote part of China - one who has plenty of expertise but few local patients - could serve these sites remotely (with a web-based translator service as the intermediary.)

- A team of Indian Ayurvedic physicians could service thousands of patients worldwide, all from one internet-based healing center based in India.

- The herbs could be grown in the local community and filed away using a numbering system, so if the doctor prescribes specific quantities of herbs 3, 29 and 47 mixed in tea, a local elder could mix the herbs and administer them to the patient. It's not the best of all solutions, but it could save a tremendous amount of lives.

Therefore, we believe that creating a Medical Remedies Team as a division of WHT would be a welcome addition to our service in the poorest parts of the world.

Chapter 30 - The Role of Technology & Science

Management of Crops via Data Capture and Dissemination

Ask any group of farmers the key to maintaining high levels of crop output, and they will tell you the same thing: understanding the needs of the plants in terms of light, temperature, nutrients, water and pest control; letting nature meet those needs where possible, and supplementing them when nature does not. There is a well-documented science to growing food. Implementation is not always easy or affordable, but farmers around the world know and understand the basics of traditional plot farming.

However, greenhouse farming will be new to the majority of these people. This means that their previous outdoor farming experience will provide little help in solving the unique challenges the WHT greenhouses will present.

The goal of WHT as a scientific growing community is to harness and share the knowledge of hundreds, thousands and millions of farmers, botanists, scientists and engineers from around the world. No fact is too simple, no technology too complex, when you have experts from all backgrounds speaking a common language. The common language we share is concern and love for our fellow human beings. Each of the participants in WHT wants to grow the best food, in the highest quantity and quality, for the lowest cost, in the quickest way possible.

How do we share this knowledge with facilities as far away as southern Africa, as remote as the jungles of Belize, as isolated as a tiny village 300 miles from the nearest city in Mexico? And how do we capture data and input from the field - when the field is literally every remote point on the planet?

The answer, of course, is the internet. That is why **in the**

advanced phases of our WHT rollout, we want to share the collective knowledge of our facilities on a worldwide basis, by linking the facilities electronically.

We need a way to get simple computers in place at each facility, powered by solar cells, linked to the web via a satellite hookup. I'll leave it to the techies to figure out how to make this happen, but it's the obvious and logical key to making the information sharing system work.

To achieve this, every WHT collection facility will need three things:

1. Internet access.
2. A computer.
3. A digital camera.

Internet access will be required to communicate with the 'mother ship' - WHT headquarters. Why is this critical? Because the local community will have ongoing needs. They will tell us what is working and what is not, they will tell us their problems and concerns, and they will transfer new knowledge and techniques they have developed that work for them. All of this knowledge will be captured and analyzed, and the beneficial items will be added to our collective knowledge base. In this way, current and future WHT communities will have a running start at avoiding the same problems and solving the same issues quickly.

A computer will be needed in all WHT communities to interface with the internet, obviously. But it will also be critical to record planting dates, harvesting dates, crop yields, etc., as well as information about the facility in general. In many installations, a translator service will be required so that the residents of the WHT facility can communicate in their native tongue, with their comments translated into English to share with the WHT team.

A digital camera will be needed to show the results of the team's effort in the WHT facility. Successes need to be shared, as well as problems. The experts in each area will need to see detailed photographs of the works in progress so they can better determine their prognosis and solutions. Team members and donors back in the states will need to see results to keep them motivated, and help them build an emotional connection to the people benefiting from their efforts.

Electricity, Networking and Satellite Hook-Up

Of course, before we can even begin to talk about establishing this internet hook up of remote installations, we will need some infrastructure in place. Computers and networks require electricity, and the WHT installations will require a substantial number of solar panels and electrical storage batteries. Great strides have been made in both of these areas of technology, greatly reducing their cost while increasing their efficiency.

In addition, we will need to network the WHT installations to the internet via a satellite connection. We are confident that a joint effort of technology companies could establish this communications network. With proper design and planning, the system can be made extremely user-friendly and easy to maintain.

Once this internet interface is in place, we will use it to link the expertise of thousands of consultants in technology-rich nations with farmers and greenhouse operators located in WHT installations around the world.

Ultra-Identification To Keep Everything Organized

As we roll-out hundreds and even thousands of greenhouses around the world, how will we keep them all straight? We believe that a very sophisticated and organized data identification scheme will be needed. It may sound complicated, but it will actually make things much simpler in the long run.

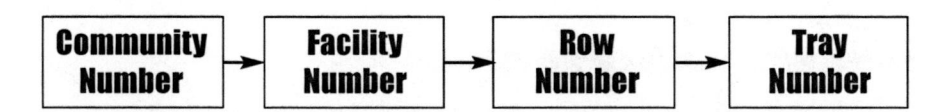

Community Number	→	Facility Number	→	Row Number	→	Tray Number

1. Identification. Each WHT growing community will have a unique community number. Each growing facility (greenhouse) within that community will have a unique facility number. Within each facility will be rows upon rows of growing trays; each row will have a unique identification number. Along the row will be individual growing beds or trays, i.e. individual plastic container holding one or more units of a particular plant; each tray will have a unique tray number. All of this information will be printed on a unique permanent-adhesive / waterproof / barcoded tray tag. With one scan, we will be able to bring up the entire history of this tray, what crop is currently growing in it, what issues have been identified with the tray, crop yield, etc.

The Program That Links It All Together

We will also need a master program that remote users can access to record and monitor the growing cycles of the plants in their greenhouses. For example, the biology experts that are a part of WHT will determine the exact number of days in the productive life of a plant. They will have expert knowledge on when to plant specific crops, when to fertilize them, when to trim back the shoots, when to transplant, and when to pull them and replant. They'll know all of this, and they'll have specific days that things need to happen.

The key fact to consider is that the people doing the actual planting and greenhouse care and maintenance down in Belize will have no way of knowing what days that things need to happen. They'll be 'shooting in the dark' and trying to do what they THINK is right. This process of trial and error may be entirely WRONG for the health and success of the food crop. So that is why we need a computer-based system that monitors the crops, by type of crop, by greenhouse ID #, and by greenhouse tray.

The System Maximizes The Growing Cycle

Let's say we have a greenhouse in Belize that has been designated for growing green beans. Here's how we will keep track of our effectiveness or inefficiencies in this greenhouse:

- The greenhouse has an identification number of "1019". Inside greenhouse 1019 are 50 growing beds (made of recycled plastic, of course).

- Each of these trays has an identification number of "1019-01" through "1019-50".

- On day one, the system tells the workers to plant green bean seeds in trays 01 through 10.

- They are told to wait 10 days, then plant seeds in trays 11 through 20, wait another 10 days and then plant seeds in trays 21 through 30, etc.

- The workers are wondering, "why not plant ALL of the seeds in ALL of the trays on day one? Wouldn't that produce the most food in the shortest amount of time? But the system knows better: it knows that to output the most food, you need plants in different life stages at different times of the year. It means that when trays 01 through 10 are reaching maturity and no longer yielding food, trays 41 through 50 are in full output mode.

The system can guide the workers, so there IS NO LEARNING CURVE to growing the maximum amount of food. Sure, there will unique circumstances and knowledge to be gleaned from the field workers. This all needs to be captured on a daily basis, and sent to the home office for collection and processing.

As we learn more about the real-world implementation issues, the more we can tweak the system. A problem that was solved by the workers in Belize can be transmitted to the home office, and relayed to facilities around the world. Similarly, problems that are experienced in Southern Africa may be solved by workers in Northern Canada.

Why Do We Need A System - Can't We Just Let The Farmers Grow Food ?

In a normal farming situation, the farmers can determine what their crops need. But as I mentioned at the start of this chapter, many of the WHT facility operators will never have grown crops in a greenhouse environment. The plants in the greenhouse will be affected by the same factors that affect outdoor crops, i.e. moisture levels, temperature, light, oxygen, nutrients, soil pH, bugs / pests, disease, etc. But their identification and control will require _different skills and solutions_ than with traditional farming.

Many of these factors will be unseen to the naked eye. If the greenhouse manager / farmer is inexperienced in the art of identifying the problem with a particular growing bed, he or she can often compound the problem by taking incorrect steps to correct it. Farmers may add more water when the problem is soil pH, and the net result is further degradation of the plant. They may add more fertilizer when the problem is disease, and the net result is that the plant is burnt up by over-fertilization. These types of issues will only reduce or completely negate the production of food in that particular growing tray.

Let The Plants Tell Us What's Wrong

To solve this problem, we propose the use of individual data collection sensors that will be inserted into each growing tray.

- **The bottom tip of the sensor** will collect data to monitor the soil conditions as well as temperature below the ground.

- **The exposed middle of the sensor** will have a light sensor that will collect ambient light readings as well as air temperature.

- **The top of the sensor** will have a miniature camera that will take low-resolution digital photographs of the plants throughout the day.

Each of these sensors will be linked by hard wires which lead to the outer wall of the greenhouse. All of the wires will terminate at a master data control box. This data control box will have a simple microprocessor inside that compiles the data and writes it to a digital hard drive. The greenhouse manager / farmer will have a laptop computer that plugs into the master data control box with a standard Ethernet cable.

The data is uploaded into the facility operating program and added to the history of that particular greenhouse. Each day, the greenhouse manager / farmer logs onto the internet via satellite dish, and the data is uploaded to the master WHT operating program.

The net output of these sensors will provide virtually all of the information that an experienced botanist / farmer will need to identify:

a. *Current health / age / growth cycle of the plant*
b. *Existing conditions of the growing environment*
c. *Specific and exact factors that are inhibiting the health and productivity of the plant*
d. *Specific and exact corrective action that is required to return the plant to full efficiency*

Action Plan by Individual Tray. After the data is analyzed and discussed, a specific action plan is relayed via the internet to the greenhouse manager / farmer.

He or she will use this data to take exact and specific steps on a tray-by-tray basis to correct the unique problems present in each tray.

The advantages of this system are many:

a. All of the worldwide participants in WHT can help solve problems.
Members of the different WHT teams around the world will have read-only rights to view the data coming from all WHT installations. This means that a farmer in New Jersey may quickly identify the problems occurring in a growing facility in Botswana. The farmer in New Jersey reports his findings to the team leader of the crop in question, i.e. the Tomato Team Leader. This individual is the ultimate decision maker as to identifying the problem(s) and issuing the orders to solve the problem(s). The team leader can delegate this task to anyone on the Tomato Team. The net result is that a certified, competent expert in tomato growing will provide an action plan to the grower / farmer in Botswana, telling that person what corrective action to take on a tray-by-tray basis throughout the growing facility.

These actions will bring the collective knowledge and proven history of the entire tomato-growing community worldwide, directly to the individual farmer, directly to the specific conditions of each and every growing tray within the facility.

This removes the guesswork, the trial and error, the down-time, and the lack of food yield that can result from inefficient or poor decisions made by the farmer. In essence, the data will be available for review by any and all interested participants. Members of the Tomato Team will debate the potential solutions to problems in facilities around the world, via the Tomato Team blog. Who wins? Everyone wins.

b. **Food yield will be maximized.** By removing the trial and error of growing food, the greenhouse can reach maximum output all year round.

c. **Trends will be identified.** If the Tomato Team identifies a particular disease that is spreading across the region or the continent, specific actions can be taken in non-affected areas before the problem is even present in those areas.

d. **Every greenhouse manager / farmer will become an expert** - even if he or she has never grown a plant before.

Communication and Global Sharing of the WHT Knowledge Base

When it comes to plants and growing food, it's a given fact that someone somewhere in the world will have experienced this before, and will have knowledge to share. Our mission at WHT is to facilitate the rapid and detailed dissemination of that knowledge in an easy-to-use, step-by-step manner, which people from all educational backgrounds with all variety of cultural / ethnic / language backgrounds can understand and implement. It doesn't have to be as complicated as it sounds, either.

The online database will archive a vast array of solutions to everyday issues for each crop. In cases where no knowledge exists in the database, the problem will be disseminated among the members of the crop team - people from around the world who have registered their expertise and agreed to help solve problems relating to that particular crop. A variety of likely solutions will be produced, and the team will vote on the most likely solution and relay it to the WHT facility. If the solution proves effective, it will be added to the online database. Thus, the worldwide network will help to quickly solve problems on the local front.

Share The Knowledge On The Web - And In Person

We will establish a schedule of frequent meetings of each specialty team via a web conference. An agenda will be required, and rules of order will be put in place, (see details in Chapter 37.)

In addition, we will establish an annual national conference to share our progress worldwide. Sub-conferences and meetings of the specialty teams will take place at this same time. We will also have meetings of upper management teams at this conference, with a focus on building our participation and cooperation with other hunger relief organizations around the world.

Chapter 31 - WHT Implementation by Phases

It will be impossible to accomplish everything outlined in this book immediately, so WHT must start small and grow as time and funding allows. We propose four basic levels of implementation, as follows.

PHASE 1: JUST GROW FOOD. In the initial phase, we will set up one or more greenhouses according to the starting plan. We will grow the crops that have tested the best in terms of ease of growing and total food output, and we will start to feed the local community. In this phase, we will simply grow the food and distribute it to the local residents.

PHASE 2: COOKING. In the second phase, a commissary will be constructed by WHT to prepare, cook and serve the food to hungry residents. There will never be a charge of any kind for meals, service or ancillary products; any miscellaneous costs of operation should be minimal and will be borne by charity donations.

PHASE 3: SUPPORT BUILDINGS. In the third phase, support buildings will be constructed. These include food storage facilities, dining halls, schools, recreational facilities, and toilet / shower facilities. Here, we begin to support the daily needs of the community and add more to their daily lives and social structures.

PHASE 4: HOMES. In the fourth phase, homes will be constructed. These will be simplified single-design structures. The design will be refined over time to create the ideal living facility that requires the minimal amount of expense and maintenance, and can be constructed in the shortest time frame.

There will be further refinement of these goals as we learn more about our capabilities and resources. These categories are outlined just to give us a broad outline of what we can expect to provide in the WHT communities.

WHT Team Structure

As in the operation of any commercial enterprise, a management structure must be established to distribute and manage WHT's duties effectively. We propose to do this by:

a. Designing a simple growing facility that uses building materials composed entirely of recycled plastics

b. Assembling a team of contributing partners from all sectors of the population:

   i. **Academic**: colleges and universities will compete against one another to develop the project:
   1. *Architecture departments* create new designs and construction methods
   2. *Engineering departments* create new building products and heating / cooling / irrigation systems
   3. *Biology departments* test a wide range of growing methods and vegetable / fruit varieties

   ii. **Commercial**: companies will devote R&D research to streamline the production and manufacturing processes of the greenhouse facilities, as well as to improve the strength of the materials and the facility designs.

   iii. **Churches**: ordinary citizens will form local teams to collect, sort and verify the integrity of the collected plastic materials.

   iv. **Communities**: to reduce landfill congestion and improve the marketability of the collected plastics, cities will provide collection points for the enhanced plastic collection system.

Each member of the team, whether they be individuals or organizations or corporations, will be critical in our success. This is why the "team" concept is so critical: everyone is vital to our success and everyone has a key role in helping us achieve our goals.

Chapter 32 - Social Issues

Social Issues - United States

WHT is a team venture - organized by the people of America, and run by the people of America. It is a grass-roots effort, not a government effort. The goal of this project is to provide a viable, expandable and permanent solution to hunger. The beneficiaries will be people anywhere in the world where hunger is a problem: Africa, Haiti, South America - and even poor communities in the United States. There will never be a charge for establishing a food community. The food community will never be primarily a 'for profit' venture; surplus food may eventually be sold to local restaurants and grocers, but it is not the primary intent of the venture. Free food and sustenance will always be available to all who need it.

Social Issues - Foreign Countries

Regional Sovereignty

It is important to note the advantages of the WHT program contrasted with the traditional Peace Corps approach to solving hunger. The Peace Corps and other volunteer humanitarian organizations do a wonderful job and are very much needed in today's world. But when we as members of an assistance group set food on foreign soil, or even take up assistance residence in a neighboring community, we are guests of the locals. Regardless of their social, political or economic status, they own and permanently reside on their land. Therefore, they do not want permanent visitors to claim the territory and laud it over them; they want our assistance and they want us to leave.

The WHT solution provides a constantly evolving, growing community that provides ongoing daily assistance to the local residents. The residents will benefit from ongoing technological advances developed by WHT, and they will benefit from ongoing supplies and training by WHT. But once the core facility is functioning and the local managers have been taught to operate it, WHT will leave. Our hope is that residents will revere the rewards they have gained, and they will welcome our next visit with open arms.

Maintaining the Essence of the Community

To recap our mission, a major goal of our interaction with the local communities is to cease our day-to-day presence as quickly as possible. By doing so, the community can go back to its normal routines and be free of the presence of outsiders. There are many reasons for this necessity:

1. Leadership. The social structure must return to its normal levels, where no outsiders are making decisions for the community. We can provide the resources they need, but inevitably the local leaders must make all decisions and be the local magistrates of their communities.

2. Ownership. The local people will know that they own the WHT facility, and it is theirs to manage and enjoy. Once the community realizes that one of their own residents is in charge, the project will not be a 'charity' distribution point; it will be a locally owned and managed source of food and social interaction.

3. Support. In some cases, the residents of WHT communities will resent outside interference; that is to be expected. But once the doubters realize that the facility is producing quality food that is distributed for free, we hope to make some headway in overcoming their resistance. Eventually, they may realize that there is no 'free lunch', and that growing the food requires hard work on the part of volunteers, as well as the support and protection of the local citizens. Over time, the original opponents may become the strongest supporters of the WHT facility.

As the needs of their local community grow, we hope that all of the local residents recognize the value of the contribution that WHT has made to their community. Hopefully, this will lead to their being receptive to participating in the global experiment of WHT. By having loyal advocates within the native community, we hope that these individuals can dialogue with the naysayers and eventually convince them of the value of interacting with the worldwide WHT community.

Friend or Competitor?

A core level issue that will certainly arise is the reaction of the local farming community. If a farmer makes his or her living growing crops for the local villages, and we distribute the same crops for free, what becomes of the farmer's livelihood? We can cause more harm than good to this individual. The overall community is better served because sustenance will no longer be reserved for the privileged few who have an income - it will be provided to all, regardless of their income. Accommodating the farmer and his or her financial stability is a key issue in areas of mixed economic need. The WHT organization will have to address difficult issues such as these as problems arise.

Local Politics

Another potential problem will be local politics. Consider the problem that has plagued Rwanda for generations: the Hutu and Tutsi regimes have killed each other for years, for no key reason other than their different origins. If we built a facility serving the Hutu community, the Tutsi people would want to destroy it.

We are aware that we will certainly lose facilities over these concerns, but as an organization there is probably little we can do about it. Therefore, our motto will be, move on / move ahead, and write off our losses. The cost of the original facility is not large enough that we should lose sleep - or lives - in attempting to retake the captured facility.

Chapter 33 - WHT Participation Roles

The Role of Elementary, Middle and High Schools

Schools have been trying to drum home the message of ecological responsibility since the first 'Earth Day' in 1970. What better way to get kids involved in helping to save our planet than to get them actively involved in hands-on recycling? Of course, recycling programs have been in place for many, many years and they have made a tremendous impact on our planet. But there is so much more that can be done.

We propose getting the grade schools involved in teaching kids the different recycling numbers, as well as having them become WHT 'Plastic Sheriffs' that wash, sort and bag the recyclable plastic materials. If these kids develop a strong sense of involvement in the proper sortation and collection of plastics, they will become better protectors of our environment as well as concerned and involved citizens of the world.

The Role of Colleges and Universities

Colleges and universities will play a huge role in the growth and success of WHT. Everything about our organization and operation is 'open for discussion', so we will constantly need new ideas, new concepts to test, new structures to build and refine. The students of today are the leaders of tomorrow, and as more students get involved in taking an active daily role in directly participating in the needs of the world community, we will begin to actively solve these problems.

Some competition will be good in this regard. Let's say that we have an annual national contest to design, build and implement a new greenhouse design. Rules will be established to level the playing field, and the winner will be decided by the maximum output of any individual crop category. In other words, the total 31-day output by weight of tomatoes divided by the square footage of the greenhouse, will determine the winner in the tomato category. Repeat the same contest for squash, green beans, melons, etc., and you can see how we will have dozens if not hundreds of agricultural schools competing to find the absolute best way to grow these crops in a greenhouse environment.

The schools will enlist the support of their architecture and engineering teams to help design the facilities. They will enlist the biology and botany departments, as well as the home economics and industrial trade departments. Participating in the WHT program could become a 'feather in the cap' of today's leading educational institutions, and the world will benefit from their valuable contributions.

The Role of Retirees and Experienced Volunteers

There is a tremendous wealth of talent to be found among the senior citizens of our nation, and much of this talent is greatly under-utilized today. Far too often, the employers of our nation overlook these talented individuals in favor of hiring young people. While these young people have much-needed energy and vitality, they often lack the expertise and well-developed skills that are second nature to the mature adults.

Example #1. Consider the skills of a 70-year-old woman living in a small community in the Midwest. She has devoted her life to growing the biggest, most bountiful tomato crop in the state. She has won many accolades such as the blue ribbon at the state fair; her techniques and tips have been published numerous times in the county newspaper. But her children have grown and moved away, and nobody in her family or social community has shown an interest in continuing her work. She is a veritable walking encyclopedia in the 'do's and don'ts' of growing tomatoes, yet her life's work will disappear if nobody is there to access it.

This woman could be a valuable contributor to the WHT Tomato Team.

Example #2. Let's suppose that as the WHT Architectural Team begins to test the temperature variations in the greenhouse caused by moving air through the underground air chambers, they experience some unanticipated humidity issues. Short of installing a dehumidifier or some complicated equipment that would not be viable in the remote WHT locations, the team has hit a stalemate.

A retired building engineer decides to poke around on the Team's website and reads about the problem. He posts a short 2 sentence reply on their blog, explaining that in 1965 his company had the same problem in a cold storage facility and they installed a certain type of air return chamber that fixed the problem. Stunned at the simplicity of the solution, the Team has saved months or even years of testing, and they arrive at a viable solution within days - based solely on the retiree's comments.

Suffice it to say that given the breadth and depth of experience that today's senior citizens have been through, there are experts galore with plenty of knowledge to lend. It will be beneficial to these talented individuals to find a resource that is appreciative of their knowledge - and it will be beneficial to the success of WHT to tap into this wealth of knowledge to find answers to complex problems.

The Role of the Military

The U.S. Armed Forces are among the top strategic and logistic experts in the world. If you need to deliver 5 tons of supplies to a specific set of coordinates by a specific time, ask the military to do it. The items will be on the spot at the exact time specified - no questions asked, no doubt as to whether it will be done.

WHT sees a huge role for the military in helping us achieve our goals. After all, they already send ships, planes and vehicles to points throughout the world; why not have them move WHT materials when they have excess capacity? This is one area in which we will be asking for government help in achieving our goals. We're not going to be asking for a handout; we're going to be asking for a partnership.

Should we successfully negotiate a working partnership with the U.S. government, we see a true win/win relationship. The U.S. has a vested interest in seeing foreign aid actually invested in the future stability of assisted nations, rather than lost in the maze of foreign bureaucracy.

Domestic Participation - Unemployed & Underemployed Citizens

Tens of millions of Americans are now out of work or underemployed. Many of these individuals have lost their jobs due to foreign outsourcing or the shift of manufacturing jobs to Mexico or China. These are valuable, educated people who need a new career or at least a new source of food and shelter for their families. Tent cities are forming across the nation, and these people often have little hope of getting ahead.

WHT can play a key role in rehabilitating the lives of these citizens, as we build new WHT communities across America. Rather than providing soup kitchens to nourish these individuals for one day, we propose building social centers around which these people can build a life. They can contribute to and be a part of something huge, something that helps everyone, including themselves.

As discussed in Chapter 11, the Works Progress Administration (WPA) of the 1930's employed millions of people across America in a wide range of service jobs across all sectors of human life. This was a government-funded program to get America back on its feet again and provide a way for people to find gainful employment and training in their chosen field.

Similar to the efforts of the WPA but on a far smaller scale, the WHT can serve as a focal point to bring people together around a common cause: solving world hunger.

The primary premise will be to plan, design, implement and perfect a system to solve hunger in foreign nations. But the secondary goal and benefit will be to provide a life center and nutrition for America's under-served and under-nourished population.

Tackling a project of this scale will require corporate funding and participation. It will take the involvement of U.S. governments at all levels: city, county, state and federal.

Corporations can participate by funding the construction of greenhouses within a local community. They can also help by funding the purchase of materials, purchase of tools and dies required to manufacture the buildings, sponsorship of plastics thermoforming companies that will make the materials, etc.

Due to stringent building codes here in the states, we do not propose 'starting from scratch' in our U.S.-based facilities. There are plenty of vacant older buildings that can be restored to house these operations. We will seek out buildings that have plenty of adjacent open land on which to construct our greenhouses. In this way, the primary facilities will already meet the local codes; we will simply need to work with the local municipalities to meet codes on the greenhouse structures that will be built and operated on the surrounding land.

Although there are many fine food relief efforts in place here in the states, the need - unfortunately - is far outpacing the ability of these organizations to provide all of the help that is needed. We believe that these organizations will welcome the assistance of WHT. They recognize, as do we, that relief efforts cannot be a one-time solution; they must provide a path toward a permanent solution that will eventually eradicate hunger in our nation. We believe that the World Hunger Team can play a valuable role in helping these excellent organizations achieve this goal once and for all.

Chapter 34 - National Database of Recyclables

Have you ever purchased a container of juice or a bottle of shampoo and wondered what type of plastic the container was made out of? I certainly have! In some cases, the bottle is obviously made of #1 PETE, but the cap is a total mystery. Most caps are made of #5 polypropylene, but once in a while you'll get a hard plastic cap that has no number printed on it. Do you just throw it away, or do you try to recycle it? Remember that very few recycling centers collect #5 plastic - and nobody collects "mystery" plastic... (HINT: to find out where you can recycle #5 plastic as well as the other numbers that most communities don't collect, visit www.earth911.org)

That is why we propose the development of a massive, searchable online database of all plastic packaging material used in the United States. Plastics sorters will have access to this database. If they have a particular bottle or cap that is not marked with the standard recycling symbol - or if they just aren't sure about a particular item - they can log into the database, type in a portion of the product's name - i.e. 'Golden Goop Shampoo' - and every known container for this product line will come up, with a large diagram showing the correct recycling number for each element of the container. In this way, there can be no confusion as to which part goes into which recycling bin.

If an item is NOT found in the database, the volunteer is asked to photograph it and submit all product details to WHT HQ. The item will be researched and added to the database. Meanwhile, the volunteer is told to put the item in the 'mixed plastics' bin.

We believe that the manufacturers will jump through hoops to make sure all of their containers are in the WHT database. Corporate America is under intense pressure to demonstrate that they are "green." What was once a novelty is now seen as a critical component of survival in the years ahead. Today's generation not only expects their products to be biodegradeable and recyclable, they are demanding it.

Can you imagine the advertising and PR value to a major consumer products company in stating "all of our containers are WHT compliant?" Eventually, the sorters will be able to tell at a glance which items belong in which bins, but it will be important that accuracy be maintained. We propose that the sorters have permanent markers that they write the number on, whenever an item needs to be checked. In this way, the final accuracy checkers will know that the questionable items have been researched and verified. It means that the bag marked "#5 plastic" will contain 100% #5 plastic - with no variation to pollute the mix and negate the viability of the material.

Of equal importance is the need to standardize and improve the labeling of all plastic packaging materials here in the U.S. We need larger, clearer numbers on all items. Anyone and everyone should be able to tell at a glance whether a detergent bottle is made up of #2 plastic or #5 plastic, and whether the cap is made of #4 or #5 plastic. Why are so many plastic packaging items today completely unlabeled?

Despite the many benefits of labeling, many of the top manufacturers could actually fight this system. That is because it will cost them additional funds for re-tooling, and it could force them to start using different and more expensive materials in the manufacturing of their packaging.

However, it's really the U.S. consumer who holds all of the power: we can make or break a product through our **purchasing power**. If one manufacturer is able to label its products as 100% recycling compliant and another manufacturer refuses to do so, we as consumers can 'vote' with our buying power. Soon, all consumer products manufacturers will see the value in being a 'green' partner to the advanced recycling / plastics reclamation efforts of an informed nation.

Chapter 35 - WHT Operating Philosophy and Ethical Platform

Operating Philosophy

WHT is a simple organization, with simple goals. We are team of dedicated individuals united under a single cause: to stop world hunger. We will accomplish this by constantly improving and simplifying the solution to make the greatest impact on the community level, with the least possible effort, the lowest cost of operation, and the simplest and fastest implementation solutions. We are 100% focused on the solution, and every one of our team members is a senior-level contributor with an eye on improving the solution. There are individuals who are in charge of managing specific departments and activities, but everyone has an equal voice in contributing ideas and opportunities to the team.

WHT is not an agent for political, social, or religious change. We are strictly a grass-roots organization united for nutritional change. Our goal is not to change laws or policies or become a branch of any government; our goal is to provide food to families who have none - and who have little hope of finding food in the future given the current state of their surroundings.

The lack of food can be caused by a myriad of reasons: the local economy, the environment, the water supply, the soil condition, lack of farming equipment, lack of experience or training, or even political conditions. WHT has one goal and one goal only: to grow regionally-appropriate food on a large-scale, consistent basis, regardless of the conditions, regardless of the location, regardless of the financial / religious / political / ethnic / cultural status of the people in need. We feed people who have no food. That is all we do, and all we will ever do.

While we will be appreciative of politicians and other individuals who will rally to support us, they will simply be members of the team. A high-ranking official who supports and helps WHT is no more important than the handicapped person in a wheelchair who sorts plastic; they are equal members of the team.

WHT members promote the goals and activities of WHT; they do not call attention to themselves or promote outside activities while 'on the job' at WHT. Neither do they link their activities at WHT to any outside cause or activity, either political or commercial. Everything a WHT member does and says relative to WHT, while at home or on the job or while traveling, should be in the interest of furthering the team efforts. Of course, team members have their own lives and activities; they simply do not promote other products, organizations or ideals while they are promoting WHT.

A good rule of thumb is this: if you are planning to attend a rally or other event for another organization or cause, don't wear your WHT T-shirt. If you are planning to go shopping on a Saturday afternoon, it's perfectly okay to wear your WHT T-shirt. If a local camera crew happens to be interviewing people at random at the farmer's market you are attending, it's okay to appear on camera. But out of deference to your teammates and the non-affiliated cause you have chosen to be a part of, do not discuss non-WHT causes or politics when you are displaying a WHT logo; it doesn't help the cause.

Because of the potential for misinterpretation of our mission, WHT does not endorse political candidates or politically-charged causes. We appreciate other people and groups, but we do not use the resources of WHT to further any other group's cause, or those of individual members of WHT; it carries too much potential for distracting from our cause.

It is critically important, therefore, that all WHT volunteers and representatives understand our position:

- WHT is an organization of people.

- WHT believes in helping people in the long term, by providing the means to grow food.

- WHT is focused on the future well being of mankind as a whole.

- WHT is not a political organization, nor will it ever be a political organization.

Anyone can join the team and call themselves a WHT team member or participate in a WHT facility; our doors will be barred to no man, woman or child. We invite people to be a part of WHT regardless of race, creed, color, age, gender, employment status, citizenship status, lifestyle status, domicile status, organizational membership status or employment status.

We do not discriminate against anyone for any reason. If you are willing to assist us in our mission in any way, shape or form, you are invited and welcome to be a part of WHT. All are invited to share in the sowing and the reaping of our harvest. All we ask is that you make at least one effort per week - however small, toward furthering our goal to feed the hungry. The effort can be as small as saving one plastic container for plastic reclamation; it can be as large as devoting your every waking minute to the cause.

In many communities that we serve, the WHT facility will become the town center or city hall. As such, WHT will never block our doors to any meeting of the people, for any group or cause - however laudable or personally deplorable. The facilities that are constructed by WHT will belong to the people of the community. They are to be operated as free, non-profit facilities devoted to meeting the needs of the community. As long as they are operated freely and continue to support the needs of the community, they will continue to enjoy the ongoing benefits and support of WHT.

WHT will certainly catch flak over our non-aligned position. (I'm sure Switzerland caught flak in the early days as well.) To put it into perspective, let's make one thing perfectly clear: the world has been woefully negligent in addressing the food needs of the less fortunate. Shame on us as a civilization to put so little emphasis on providing for the needy. Shame on us as individuals for allowing world hunger to grow at an appalling pace. And heaven praise each and every one of us who is willing to do one thing - ANYTHING - to put an end to the suffering. That is why WHT will always welcome any donation of support, and any action on the part of any individual, organization or company, that will speed recovery to the neediest areas of the globe.

If our actions can deliver tomatoes to dying people in Darfur, any action or effort that allows us to grow tomatoes and distribute them into the hands of dying people one day quicker is a good action. Many of the starving people of the world do not have a one-day margin for error. If the emaciated and dying man at the front of the food line does not get the tomato today, his body will cease to operate; his brain will lack the essential nutrients it needs to continue to function, and his brain synapses will cease to occur. Quite simply, he will die on the spot.

If the detractors of WHT want to halt or interrupt our actions, we invite them to apply for a job as a 'tomato snatcher'. You can stand at the front of the food line and deny that man his tomato. You can proclaim a 'higher cause' or some justification for denying that man his life. Please, take the tomato out of his hands, eat it yourself, or hand-deliver it to another person or organization you deem 'more worthy'.

We don't think any such person or group exists. But if you DO, you can stand there and watch the man die and explain to the world why you were "in the right."

Not realistic? Not accurate? Not a fair representation? Unfortunately, it's extremely accurate, and it's happening every day, around the world. We just want to stop it. What do YOU want to do about it?

Chapter 36 - Purpose in Life

While our #1 goal is to stop world hunger, our #2 goal is to give our team members a purpose in life. Everyone needs to feel important, to feel needed and to be of value, a contributor to some organization, group or cause. WHT gives every individual, of every age, of every income, of every skill level or talent, the chance to be an equal and vital contributing member of a worldwide organization.

Whether that individual is a multi-millionaire or a homeless person who does not know where his or her next meal is coming from, they are welcome at WHT.

Whether they are eating food from WHT because it's part of a social activity, or whether they have no other source of food, they are welcome at WHT.

WHT can operate in the rec room of a senior center; it can operate in the basement of a church; it can operate in a member's garage, it can operate anywhere. There is no single location of WHT, other than in the hearts of its' members.

Recipient or Participant: They Are One and The Same

Pride is a funny thing; many a man or woman would rather starve than admit he needs assistance. If a person has come to 'a certain age', he wants to feel proud of his life's accomplishments. Everyone wants the world to view them as a success, someone who has mastered life's challenges and risen to a secure position for himself and his family. But what happens to that individual when the factory he has worked at for 30 years closes, and the company has moved away or folded - taking his pension money with it. Often there are no jobs to be had, and after a while the unemployment runs out. Does this once-proud individual gladly go 'on the dole' and ask the government to provide for him? Very typically, no - he is too proud and too embarrassed to be in this situation this late in life. One look at the growing homeless situation in this country will verify this to be true. And this is where WHT can help most of all.

We hope to have WHT test sites in many U.S. cities. The premise of these sites is that every volunteer is helping to test and perfect the system for worldwide rollout. And this is a true and accurate statement.

The goal of WHT test sites will be to:
   a. *Implement the food growing process in a variety of environmental conditions*
   b. *Test new ideas*
   c. *Generate new ideas for growing, storing and preparing food*
   d. *Test new building concepts and designs*
   e. *Monitor the results at each location and share them along the WHT network for others to learn from*

A 55-year-old homeless man could generate the best ideas and results, or they could originate from a 5th grade class at the local elementary school. Every man, woman and child alive today has a different set of skills and experiences, and everyone can bring something to the table.

A classic story comes to mind: a semi-truck is stuck under a bridge, and the 'experts' are trying to figure out how to remove it. A passing child suggests letting air out of the tires, and the method works. Just as the child sees a different solution to the problem, people with no known training in a specific discipline can come up with remarkably insightful solutions to complex needs.

There are always many different views of how to solve a problem, and we cannot predict where the best answers will come from.

That is why we want to encourage everyone in a community, regardless of their current status or expertise, to become a WHT team member. Becoming a team member is a little like getting a job, but without cash compensation. Team members will receive compensation in other ares of their lives:

• A warm, welcoming place to spend time.

• A friendly atmosphere where they can contribute their efforts toward a good cause.

• An open and encouraging environment where their opinions will have merit, and their efforts will reap tangible, visible gains.

• Access to the WHT food output and / or meals prepared in the WHT on-site kitchen.

• The chance to be part of something really, really big - a chance to make a difference in the world, starting in your own community.

Whether the individual is helping to build facilities, grow the food, prepare the food, or maintain the premises - every WHT member will be welcome to free food and meals. Everyone can eat, whether they live in a million dollar mansion or under a railroad bridge. And everyone can maintain their pride and deny that they need the free food. They can claim that "it's just easier to eat here" than to go home and cook. There is no loss of pride or judgment passed down on you when you share meals with your friends at WHT. Rather, each participating individual will gain respect and self-worth for devoting his time and energy towards a noble cause.

Nobody cares about how much money you bring to WHT, because no money will change hands in a WHT facility - _ever_. In all U.S. facilities, all donations are to be mailed to a WHT lock box at a local bank. We will NEVER have a cash collection box in any WHT installation, simply because we do not want to restrict participation to those with money.

Every ounce of food grown in a WHT facility will be consumed by the local team members, or distributed by the team members for free to needy individuals and institutions. In the event that a WHT facility out-produces the needs of the local community, it can establish a commercial venture to sell the food product to restaurants or grocery stores, but never at the expense of taking food away from the needy.

Our purpose in life is clear: we feed people, by developing and perfecting the means to grow, prepare and distribute food. Nature does the hard work of growing the food; we simply improve the conditions for Nature to "do its thing."

Chapter 37 - WHT Rules of Order

Questions / Comments / Open Forums

It is inevitable that there will be people who have significant comments, questions or complaints about WHT. In public forums, the response could range from elation to outrage. That is why we are proposing that all discussion forums require Q&A participants to structure and preface their comments in advance into one of three categories, and to minimize their query into maximum one-minute statements such as:

1. **I NEED CLARIFICATION ON A WHT POSITION.**

2. **I WANT TO HELP WHT**, and I have a suggestion for an improvement.

3. **I DISAGREE WITH THE WHT APPROACH**, and here is the summary of my greatest concern or comment.

This should minimize the sheer volume of words required to process the request, plus it will simply make it easier to understand where each participant is coming from.

In the event that a question or comment CANNOT be effectively conveyed in a one-minute statement, the participant will be asked to complete a **MAJOR PLATFORM STATEMENT (MPS)** and submit it to the meeting organizers. At the end of the Q&A session, the summary statements from the MPS form will be read, and the committee will determine what action needs to be taken on the item. If the action request can be dealt with on a local level, the WHT organizers will answer the request immediately if possible or determine who should handle the request locally. If the action is too complicated or large, the request will be sent 'upstream' to WHT national headquarters, (WHT HQ.)

The response from WHT to any and all questions or comments needs to be structured into one of the following three replies:

1. **YOUR INPUT IS NOTED** and will appear in the notes of our meeting, which will be routed to WHT HQ for possible action.

2. **YOUR INPUT REQUIRES DOCUMENTATION** due to its complexity. Please complete a COMMENT DETAIL form so that the appropriate people within WHT can process and /or take action on your input.

3. **PLEASE VOLUNTEER TO IMPLEMENT YOUR SUGGESTION by filling out a VOLUNTEER COMMITMENT FORM** telling us what you are willing to commit to in the way of help. The question we will pose back to people who disagree with our approach and / or believe they have a better way to go about things, is: "Will you join WHT and help us implement the improvements you are suggesting?"

We believe in this so strongly, we will literally make you a WHT consultant in 5 minutes or less. We will have registration forms and temporary business cards available at all WHT meetings; simply register as a consultant, and you will BE a consultant. You will be entitled to order a supply of permanent business cards from our 3rd party vendor, and you will become part of the team in your chosen category of expertise. If you want to share your knowledge, we want to make it very easy for you to participate.

What's more, if you DO choose to participate and continue contributing for a full 12 months, you will become a senior consultant. How about that? You probably won't make any money, but at least you'll have a title...!

We Have Met The Management, And They Are Us

It is important to note that WHT is not a typical organization that has management and employees; there is no hierarchy of administration. There is no "they" or "them" to whom questions or comments are directed; there is only "us". In other words, everyone may have an opinion of how to address the hunger issue. Everyone may want to change the way WHT operates, what locations are served, who gets first attention, how the organization is managed, etc.

Of course, ideas will come along that can only be implemented in the field. If you are a Fortune 500 executive in Manhattan, you may have a great idea for soil treatment in the Saharan Desert. Nobody will expect you to actually go there to start treating the soil; that would not be practical. And that is why the DOCUMENTATION option should be followed here. That same executive may be able to volunteer some of his staff to document and research the idea; that is what we mean by "rolling up your sleeves." By doing so, this executive will be making a positive impact on the solution, rather than just passing on random ideas hoping that "they" will implement them. Again, there is no "they" in WHT; there is only "us".

WHT Corporate Structure - Private Organization Status

WHT is a private organization, and it must remain a private organization. Why is this so, you might ask. With all of the resources of the federal government, why not make it a government-led organization so it can grow quicker?

The problem with government-led institutions is that bureaucracy inevitably seeps in. What was once a motivated and efficient team becomes a bureaucratic beehive with layers upon layers of management officers and 'consultants'. Also, purchasing supplies or selecting vendors becomes a political issue, and 'budget allocations' become a way to reward friends and reap personal rewards.

We need a lean and austere management group that finds ways to get things done as cheaply, quickly and efficiently as possible. That is why we will always be independent and not aligned with any government entity.

Chapter 38 - WHT Financials

Here are some of the financial implications that will face WHT as we start to grow.

a. Is WHT a sustainable concept?

b. How much recyclable plastic is available, and how much can one organization realistically process?

c. How can costs be held to the absolute lowest factor possible, so maximum food output can be achieved for the least amount of cash?

d. The cheaper the building, the more buildings we can implement. How inexpensively can these buildings be manufactured, and how structurally sound will they actually be?

e. Once these buildings are in place, what is their long-term viability? How much maintenance and re-engineering will they need over time?

f. Converting cash into compassion: if WHT comes into huge amounts of cash through donations or corporate sponsorships, how quickly can we 'ramp things up' to make a greater impact on the world?

g. Conversely, what if corporate America and the major foundations of the world give WHT a big yawn, and collectively decide that the concept is not viable? How will we raise funds in this tight economy?

h. What is the quickest, simplest and most effective way to solve world hunger, given all of the conditions and limitations we will encounter?

i. As WHT grows into a large-scale organization, how can we prevent corruption and loss?

j. How can we maintain the lowest cost of operation while maintaining the highest levels of effectiveness?

k. What about competition from local businesses and farmers in the restored community? Once hunger and day-to-day survival are no longer a factor, how will WHT blend into the everyday life of the community?

l. Will local businesses find the WHT sites competitive and seek to destroy them?

m. Can local WHT communities become for-profit ventures? If so, who shares the wealth?

These are just the 'tip of the iceberg' in the issues we will face over time as an organization. I won't pretend to know all the answers right now; I am simply anticipating the complexities that await us...

Chapter 39 - WHT Expanded Role: Helping the Homeless

Solving the Homeless Situation

America is in denial about our domestic homeless situation. It seems that, until we can miraculously find a few hundred billion dollars to address the issue, we will choose to officially do nothing about it. Certainly there are non-profits working tirelessly to meet the needs of these people - and we should all thank them for it. Without their help, thousands of people would suffer from malnutrition, exposure, sickness, or worse. But the efforts of these fine people and their organizations can only scratch the surface of providing the care that is needed.

I have the good fortune to travel to Las Vegas several times per year on business. To the average tourist, Las Vegas is a booming city where everyone is affluent and free-spending. But take a drive north on Las Vegas Boulevard - away from the glowing casino lights, and beyond the 'all-you-can-eat' buffets. Less than a mile or two north of the Downtown area, you will find the streets lined with tents, sleeping bags, cardboard boxes and lean-tos, all inhabited by the less-fortunate residents of the city. Here you will find hundreds of people living on the sidewalks and alleyways surrounding one of Vegas' largest soup kitchens. By staying close to the shelter, these people can feed themselves and their families 3 times a day. But what of their other needs? How healthy can it be to live on the streets, especially during the cold weather months?

<u>We can help address the needs of homeless people across America by constructing permanent shelters made of recycled plastic</u>.

We propose the construction of simple shelters using the plastic brick concept outlined in Chapter 14. These shelters will feature multiple rooms lining each wall; each room will have a locking door with a rudimentary plastic lock; the locking mechanism can be changed out easily by the shelter manager, so access can be restricted to any particular room. (In other words; the manager controls who has access to any room on any day; there is no 'ownership' of the room by the homeless person staying there on any given night.)

The rooms will be designed with a drain along the outer walls, and the floor will be angled slightly in that direction. Because the floors, walls and ceiling will be made out of plastic, the room can be hosed down and disinfected every day.

Heating and cooling will be assisted with geo-thermal air exchange as previously described. This will also induce fresh air into the structure and maintain oxygen flow. The shelters will not have running water; separate toilet block / shower buildings will be constructed for men / women / families with young children.

Additional support buildings will be constructed for laundry service, commissary / cafeteria, medical services, social support / counseling / educational services, and individual storage. In order to stay at the facility on any given night, the individuals or families will follow a fixed procedure:

- *Register at the social support service building.*
- *Obtain a key to lock their personal possessions in an individual storage room (if needed.)*
- *Obtain a pre-bundled size-labeled package of donated used clothing.*
- *Take a shower with de-lousing soap, thoroughly scrubbing hair and scalp and body.*
- *Place all personal clothing in a supplied bar-code tagged laundry bag, to be washed overnight and returned the next day.*
- *Visit the medical support building if needed.*

Upon completion of the check-in / showering process, individuals can now pick up their room key.

The **social** advantages of this system are:

- *Provide comfort and cleanliness to the individuals, allowing them to maintain their personal hygiene and pride.*
- *Provide separate gender-specific and family-based shelters to maintain personal rights and dignity.*
- *Provide nutrition, medical services, and shelter to assure the continued health of the individuals.*
- *Provide counseling to assist in returning the individuals to a place in society.*
- *Provide an opportunity for the homeless to work their way back into society. Many of the non-professional jobs required to run the shelter can be staffed by the homeless people themselves. The majority of these individuals are seeking jobs and a way to earn a living; they will be glad to work at the shelter in exchange for a reliable place to live / work / eat.*
- *Provide a central focal point for the community to address the homeless issue and support their residents who need assistance.*

The **technical** advantages of this system are:

- **Low-cost solution.** These facilities will be, in essence, simple cabins made of recycled plastic, so material costs will be low.
- **Easy to maintain.** The structures can simply be 'hosed off' and air dried. Housekeeping will be greatly simplified.
- **Construction will be simple.** The structures can be built using the homeless as laborers, with minimal expert supervision.

Of course, a natural connection would be to add World Hunger Team greenhouses to the premises, giving the homeless the opportunity to work at producing food. However, there is a down side to this: it would eliminate the desire to move on.

The fear is that the homeless would view this shelter as a commune, and never want to leave. That is why I believe the WHT facility should be located in a different part of town, away from the homeless shelter. The WHT facilities, at least domestically, should not be involved in providing long-term housing to the members. In Africa, Mexico, South America, Haiti and the many impoverished areas of the world, the need is far different; we will certainly have to provide housing in the WHT community, because no other options will exist.

Here in America, we will face two major obstacles in attempting to help the homeless situation:

1. Building codes will be much stricter, and attempting to solve the need for permanent housing will prove to be much more difficult than in less-developed countries.

2. "NIMBY" attitude, (Not In My Back Yard). Cities will be hesitant to allow the construction of homeless camps that might tend to attract people from surrounding cities.

While we believe our solution could be of great benefit to the homeless people of America, addressing these very specific needs will distract from our main goal of feeding the hungry. We will leave it up to the members of WHT to determine how we can provide the greatest assistance in this regard.

Chapter 40 - Three Start-Up Levels

It would be easy to say that we will hit the ground running and immediately roll-out the final implementation of our greenhouses and other buildings. That would be a complete pipe-dream, and one that is not likely to happen. Instead, we envision three levels of implementation, ranging from the very simple to a multi-faceted roll-out.

STEP ONE: Crawl before you walk.

In this phase, we will start with extremely, *extremely* simple structures. The goal here is to get something going in the shortest amount of time, requiring the least development, yet solving some of the problems very effectively. I would envision this to be a very simple greenhouse structure, almost a glorified lean-to. It may resemble the drawing shown in Chapter 14 - or the architects and engineers may come up with a radically different solution.

That is why we will use existing sources of commercially-produced recycled plastic to create our prototype greenhouses.

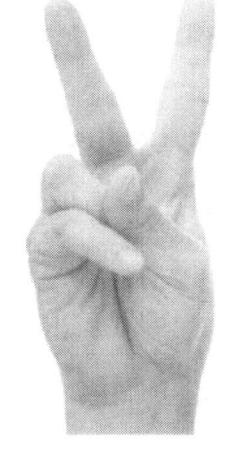

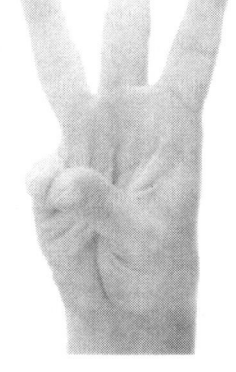

Rather than purchase expensive custom dies to produce our materials, we will use existing part designs where possible. This will keep our costs low in the testing phase and give us the flexibility to test the greatest number of designs and growing methods possible.

Whatever design we choose to start with, it will have the 'blessing' of a panel of experts who know their profession well and have given the design their utmost thought, care and concern. This will be an interim facility for us to begin testing and start the process of growing food.

STEP TWO: Walk before you run.

Here we will test a variety of advanced structures, each utilizing designs that have been tested in the university or corporate environment. There will hopefully be many designs that will be created and initially tested by the architecture and biology departments of the participating schools, as well as by concerned companies and other hunger-related organizations. We will want to replicate the most successful designs in a variety of regions and climates, growing a variety of crops to test the food yield. The results will be compared and analyzed, and one or more top designs will be refined for roll-out.

STEP THREE: Roll-out.

In the third phase we will have one or more proven greenhouse designs, or at least one design that has proven to be most flexible and productive in the field. In this final phase, we will be producing mass quantities of building materials and utilizing a fairly standardized design in the construction of our growing facilities. There will always be improvements and new test structures, but we will want to have a 'control', i.e. the one facility design that has performed best in a variety of conditions.

The future implementations of this design will surely be more productive and efficient, but the control design will continue to perform well. We will not dismantle or destroy these structures as improved designs are discovered; rather, we will simply add more of the new and improved structures to the installation site. In the areas we will be serving, land will not be at a premium; food will be at the highest premium, so we will need all of the structures, regardless of age or design, to continue their service in producing food to feed the hungry.

Chapter 41 - WHT Timetable for Implementation

Starting a new project on this scale will be difficult, to say the least. That is why we will take the traditional slow-growth approach referenced in the previous chapter.

The first goal will be to test a variety of prototype greenhouses for their effectiveness in producing high quantities of food. Simply put, the greenhouse design that we will roll out with is the one that:

a. Is the easiest design to build:

Simplicity

b. Has the lowest cost of implementation:

Economy

c. Produces the greatest output of food:

Volume

Once we have a winning design, our second goal will be to immediately begin building greenhouses in impoverished areas. Will these greenhouses be perfect? Hardly. In fact, they are likely to be very primitive. But the design that we select will have proven its ability to produce high quantities of edible food. In later years, we will surely laugh at the mistakes inherent in this initial design - but we will have been growing food and feeding starving people, and there is no mistake in that.

Only after we have reached this goal of having a winning design and are actively building greenhouses in areas of need, will we address the issue of collecting and recycling plastic. And that is our third goal: to actively seek to lower our cost of materials and increase our ability to implement the roll-out of greenhouse production through widespread collection and processing of recyclable plastic.

Why not make plastic recycling #1 in our agenda? The answer is simple, and it was explained to me by my friends at The Foundation Group in Nashville, TN, who helped us get approval for our 501(c)(3) status as a non-profit organization. When I told my representative there, Dee Hollinger, what our intentions were, she quickly corrected me. She said that we were <u>*NOT*</u> in the business of collecting plastic to recycle; we were in the business of providing an effective and sustainable way to grow food to feed the hungry in impoverished areas; the use of plastic greenhouses was simply an incidental operational tactic we would be using in our strategic goal of solving world hunger.

Think about that for a moment. Anything - and I mean anything - that we use to move from point A (the current situation whereby people are starving around the world), to point B (putting food in the hands of these starving people) - is merely a **tactic**. We will change tactics dozens - hundreds - even thousands of times in the future. The reason we will discard one tactic and pursue another, is because *we will have learned a better way to do things.*

The tactical implementations we will test involve both construction methods and growing methods.

The construction methods we will test include material selection, building design, plant bed design, trellis design, brick stability, brick translucency, UV resistance techniques, water tank design and capacity, watering methodology and equipment, testing and monitoring equipment, and hundreds of other components related to the construction and operation of the growing facilities.

The growing methods we will test include hydroponics vs. soil, natural soil vs. artificial, pollination methodology, fertilizer selection, crop selection, seed selection and hundreds of other options relating to growing plants to produce food.

And of course, we will seek to use existing knowledge bases. Our goal is to start off using the **tested and proven conclusions of the world's greatest minds.** We want to benefit from centuries of knowledge compiled by the world's greatest architects and engineers in the construction world, and the leading farmers and agricultural planners throughout history. Again, our philosophy is to not reinvent the wheel; it is to harness the best knowledge that is currently available, and to continue testing enhancements to that knowledge in our quest to improve on and economize our worldwide implementation.

How do you find out if there is a better way to do things? You test it. You receive proposals and ideas from people throughout the organization, people who are 'in the trenches' and are doing the hard work of running the day-to-day operations in each department of WHT. They propose a different approach, the idea gets floated up to the team leader, and the team leadership committee votes on which ideas deserve testing. If the challenger concept exceeds the performance of the incumbent procedure, it becomes the incumbent - and future ideas must challenge the new incumbent to become the **"control"** process. The "control" process is the current operational procedure that in active daily implementation reflects our best thinking and produces the best results.

The one thing that kills forward momentum is failing to take action until every conceivable answer is tested and approved or rejected. WHT will make mistakes, and some will inevitably be laughable in the future, but some will not; some will put tomatoes in the hands of starving children, and that is no laughing matter. It is our reason for being. And this is why we must get started as quickly as possible to implement the widespread roll-out of a satisfactory greenhouse design. I say 'satisfactory,' because we will surely create a substantially better design within months of our roll-out decision. But if we can save a small portion of the dying people in the world by taking action now, we will all be better people for it.

Chapter 42 - Call to Action: What is YOUR Role?

We believe that WHT will experience rapid growth within the first two years of implementation. Some participants will want to be aggressive while others will preach caution and restraint. The job of the leaders of WHT will be to exercise a tight balance between the two extremes: achieve quality and performance, yet roll-out a successful prototype greenhouse as quickly as possible.

Our greatest immediate challenge will be finding experts in each field. WHT is currently looking for team leaders in a variety of categories, including but not limited to:

- Irrigation
- Fertilization
- Soil
- Water
- Building Materials
- Construction
- Architecture
- Solar panels
- Thermoplastics
- Plant selection and expertise in all categories of food crops: Tomato, Cucumber, Green Beans, Lettuce, etc.
- Animal husbandry
- Housing structures
- Community buildings
- Menu planning, cooking, kitchen design and management

No aspect of creating the various WHT structures or managing the growing process will be too arcane. No aspect of running community facilities will be too large or small. Your expertise in any of these categories will be welcome at WHT.

We will start with the obvious categories and establish a team leader. All teams will have a blog that is linked to the main WHT website (www.WorldHungerTeam.com). All comments, suggestions and volunteer activity will be welcome.

Team Leader roles will be a 1-year commission. The Team Leader is expected to maintain / update / participate in the Team's blog, as well as all planning and implementation steps. Elections are held by vote of the entire team, one month prior to the commission expiration term. Commissions are honorary only, and can be revoked by the board for dereliction of duty or the good of the larger mission.

As the team grows, subcategories will arise; leaders will be needed in these subcategories, information will need to be collected, categorized, disseminated, and archived. The worldwide team could quickly grow into the thousands, and it will all require a commitment of time, energy, and knowledge.

Take this as your own personal call to action. We believe that just as WHT will serve everyone regardless of the background, participation in WHT is open to everyone. What is YOUR role? Let your mind wander to the possibilities, and then ask yourself the other question that only you can answer: What do you have to contribute? How much time can you devote to solving world hunger? When can you start?

Only you can answer these questions. But bear in mind that if you only have one hour per week or one hour per month to contribute, we value your participation. **You can make a difference.** And your contribution will be priceless to the people we serve: the starving people of the world. Your efforts can help provide them with food to eat, where now there is none. Your efforts can help save lives, and that is something that can provide significant personal rewards - a feeling of accomplishment that your time has been well spent. You will have given new life to people with little hope, and that surely is a tangible and meaningful reward for your efforts.

To start your journey in this process, please visit www.WorldHungerTeam.com and complete the participation survey. Even if you think you have nothing to offer, give us your honest answers to the questions this survey poses. You might be surprised at how much you have to offer, and how much of a difference your participation could make in the world.

Thank you for your time, and thank you for your help in creating a better, kinder world with a better future for all.

Randall Putala
Summer, 2009

Credits and Contacts

The inaugural volunteer members of the World Hunger Team, circa 2009, include (in alphabetical order):

Dale Bartholomew - Board Member, Brentwood, TN

Arthur "Bart" Bartleson - Board Member + Finance Consultant - Austin, TX

Steve Gulyas - Plastics Consultant - Marcos Island, FL

John Hreha - Book Cover Designer - Murfreesboro, TN

Dennis McEwan - Board Member + Chemical Consultant - Brentwood, TN

Deborah Scalley - Book Editor - Brentwood, TN

Isabell Shipard - Herb & Plant Consultant - Nambour, Queensland, Australia

Randall Putala - Founder and CEO - Brentwood, TN

Jeff Williams - Board Member + Construction Consultant - Brentwood, TN

To contact us, please visit www.WorldHungerTeam.com.

Final Word

There will be many revisions and updates to this book over time. If you find errors (and I'm sure there will be many) or take exception to any of the statements made in this book, (and again, I'm expecting many due to the subject matter), please report them to me by visiting our website at www.WorldHungerTeam.com. Thank you in advance for your help and sharing your knowledge.